THE WIT & WISDOM OF
MUSIC

First edition (as *The Wit & Wisdom of Music*) ©2006 House of Raven

This edition published in 2011 by Prion
An imprint of
Carlton Books Limited
20 Mortimer
London W1T 3JW

Typeset in Minion Pro and Frutiger 55
First edition design: David Coventon

ISBN: 978-1-85375-847-8

Printed in China

THE WIT & WISDOM OF
MUSIC

More than 800 amusing, enlightening
and seriously scathing quotations

PRION

A lot of people thought Rock and Roll would be a passing fancy. They were wrong. A lot of people think Rock and Roll will save the planet. They're wrong, too, whatever Bono might say.

It's just music. Much of it insipid and forgettable. But now and then you hear something and feel that little knot in the pit of your stomach uncurl and shake to the beat. And then it can be uplifting and, yes, a little inspiring.

Neil Young knew the score:
"Hey hey, my my. Rock and Roll will never die."

Contents

There are over 1,000 quotes in this collection. Each quote that appears is numbered (i.e.•123).
These numbers run sequentially throughout the book. Use the index at the back to find Rock Stars,
Pop Stars, Songwriters, Musicians, and commentators contributing to this collection. The index
is listed in alphabetical order by surname.

I think quotes are very dangerous things.

Kate Bush •1

All the good music has
already been written by
people with wigs and stuff.

Frank Zappa •2

Rock has always been
the devil's music.

David Bowie circa 1988 •3

There's no bullshit going down with rock and roll.
It's an honest form and one of the most open.
It encompasses poetry, jazz and just about anything
you can imagine… it is the highest form. It goes beyond,
colour, gender, anything. *Patti Smith,* Cashbox, 1976 •4

Have you ever wondered why young people take to music like fish to water? Maybe it's because music is fun. Plain and simple. It opens up their minds to dream great dreams about where they can go and what they can do when they get older. *Isaac Hayes* •5

> Words make you think a thought.
> Music makes you feel a feeling.
> A song makes you feel a thought.
>
> *E.Y. Harburg, lecture given at*
> *the New York YMCA in 1970* •6

> Music keeps you young — not in terms of lines or grey hairs or weight or whatever but in your spirit.
> *Paul Weller* •7

Rock and Roll is an expression of the energy of life, the energy that comes from the realization you're alive, projecting it outwards. You just wanna stamp your feet and wave your hands in the air.
Ian Astbury of The Cult 2001 •8

13

Rock and roll is the lowest form of life known to man.

Elvis Costello 1977 •9

It seemed such a sexy, pagan horror, such a dangerous new creature, that America feared it, preached against it, and tried to ban it.

Nick Tosches on rock 'n' roll •10

I love rock 'n' roll. I think it's an exciting art form. It's revolutionary. Still revolutionary and it changed people. It changed their hearts.

Nick Cave •11

Rock 'n' roll's supposed to take you away from the shit job you're in for an hour and a half and make you feel 100 feet tall.

Lemmy •12

Rock 'n' roll's never about giving up.
For me — for a lot of kids — it was a
total positive force, not optimistic all
the time, but positive. It was never,
never, about surrender.
Bruce Springsteen, 1981 •13

The best rock and roll music encapsulates a certain high
energy — an angriness — whether on record or onstage,
Rock and roll is only rock and roll if it's not safe.
Mick Jagger of The Rolling Stones circa 1981 •14

The allure of popular culture has always
been its promise of a walk on the wild side.
Cosmo Landesman •15

When you listen to good rock and roll you wanna feel fucking dirty
afterwards. You should feel so dirty you have to take a shower.
Rock and roll should be like pornography… The filthier the better.
Frank Black 1996 •16

Rock 'n' roll is like a drug. I don't take very much,
but when I do rock 'n' roll, I fuckin' do it.
But I don't want to do it all at the time 'cause
it'll kill me. *Neil Young* 1988 •17

I never thought of rock and roll as this big cultural thing
and worried about the state of it and all. It's like, plug that
fucking guitar in and give me a backseat, and 'it' lives.
Paul Westerberg ex-The Replacements 1993 •18

Rock and roll is about attitude.
I couldn't care less about technique.
Johnny Thunders 1977 •19

I don't know anything about music. I've done it all through acting.
Rock star *Meatloaf* reveals the secret of his success •20

One chord is fine,
Two chords are pushing it,
Three chords and you're into jazz.

Lou Reed circa 1975 •21

It just bores me because it's too easy.
Anyone can be that complicated. Three
notes is far cleverer than three hundred
if they're arranged in the right way, and
that's what pop music is all about.

Brett Anderson disses classical music, 1994 •22

No matter what direction rock goes
in, it has to stay with the blues.
That's the spine and body of it.

Eric Clapton •23

You're a blues person only when you're playing.
But Negro blues men live the blues environment,
eat soul food. Even hearing them talk can be like
hearing the blues. Rock is like a battery that must
always go back to blues to get recharged.

Eric Clapton 1968 •24

I can't play long solos anymore without boring myself.
Eric Clapton 2001 •25

Most people get into bands
for three very simple rock
and roll reasons: to get laid,
to get fame and to get rich.
Bob Geldof, Melody Maker, 1977 •26

The whole rock 'n' roll lifestyle?
Well, basically, we never had one.
Margo Timmins of Cowboy Junkies •27

We want to be phalluses
ramming in the butthole of pop.

Gibby Haynes of The Butthole Surfers 1993 •28

A rock 'n' roll group is a banding together of individuals
for the purpose of achieving something that none of them
can get on their own: money, fame, the right sound,
something less easy to put into words.

Greil Marcus •29

Music for the neck downwards.

Keith Richards on rock 'n' roll •30

If you look at the history of innovation in music,
it all happens by accident. Innovative music has
never come, from my perspective, from a bunch
of academics sitting around.

Moby 2001 •31

Spector, while still in his teens, seemed to comprehend the prole vitality of rock 'n' roll that has made it the kind of darling holy beast of intellectuals in the United States, England, and France.
Tom Wolfe The First Tycoon of Teen, 1965 •32

The mistake which most critics make is to persist in trying to evaluate pop culture as if it were something else: the equivalent of insisting on considering a bicycle as if it were a horse. *George Melly* Revolt Into Style (1970) •33

Rock 'n' Roll is about music.
Music. Music. Music.
It's not about you,
it's not about me,
it's not about Oasis.
It's about the songs.
Noel Gallagher, 1994 •34

Rock 'n' roll is not just music. You're
selling an attitude, too. Take away the
attitude and you're just like anyone else.
The kids need a sense of adventure and
rock 'n' roll gives it to them. Wham out
the hardest and cruellest lyrics as propaganda,
speak the truth as clearly as possible.

Malcolm McLaren •35

Younger musicians than The Sex Pistols and their peers,
the provincial ex-punks who were to start the Ska revival
of the late 1970s, would carry this golden rule with them
into the future. The first law of punk was — you can do it.
Play an instrument — you can do it. Form a band — you
can do it. Go onstage — what's stopping you?
Tony Parsons in Bare magazine in 1988 •36

When a folk club artist goes out
with his guitar, he might think
he's James Taylor or Bob Dylan.
I still think I'm The Clash.

Billy Bragg •37

A rock and roll band needs four instruments. That's a fucking fact not an opinion. As for The White Stripes, that's not rock and roll, that's performance art.

Steve Van Zandt, 2006 •38

There's always going to be the bands who change the way the river flows, and there are always going to be people who get in their boats and ride down afterwards.

Billy Corgan of Smashing Pumpkins, 1993 •39

We're like bad architecture or an old whore. If you stick around long enough, eventually you get respectable.

Jerry Garcia paraphrasing a quote from the movie, Chinatown •40

I do think rock 'n' roll should be glamorous and beautiful and sexy.

Tanya Donnelly of Belly, 1995 •41

A musician, if he's a messenger, is like a child who hasn't been handled too many times by man, hasn't had too many fingerprints across his brain.

Jimi Hendrix, in Life Magazine (1969) •42

Nothing is as important as passion. No matter what you want to do with your life, be passionate.

Jon Bon Jovi •43

That's the most Warholian thing about what I do… I embrace pop culture. The very thing that everybody says is poisonous and ostentatious and shallow, it's like my chemistry book… and I make what I believe to be art out of it.

Lady Gaga explains her philosophy to CNN •44

Music is madness. It's like a beautiful curse. When you and me are dead, man, it will still go on, which is beautiful.

Paul Weller gets all misty-eyed, March 2006 •45

All music is folk music, I ain't
ever heard no horse sing a song.

Louis Armstrong quoted in the New York Times •46

Pop music prior to the early 60s had
been purely about escapism. Escaping
from the rigours of having a humdrum
life, from living in a post-war society,
from all those things.

Pete Townshend •47

I made *Bo Diddley* in '55, they started playing
it, and everybody freaked out. Caucasian
kids threw Beethoven into the garbage can.

Bo Diddley •48

I opened the door for a lot of people and they
just ran through, and left me holding the knob.

Bo Diddley •49

Buddy Holly was the gentleman of rockabilly, the first soft rocker.

Nick Tosches •50

Either be hot or cold. If you are lukewarm, the Lord will spew you forth from His mouth.

Jerry Lee Lewis •51

I can't stand to sing the same song the same way two nights in succession, let alone two years or ten years. If you can, then it ain't music, it's close-order drill or exercise or yodelling or something, not music.

Billie Holiday **Lady Sings The Blues** (1956) •52

27

My ambition was to eat. We were very hungry.

James Brown on his childhood •53

Brown develops a number through a series of
crescendos — mounting steadily in volume, fervour
and drive — until the rising tension demands the
release of shouting and body movement. The physical
side of love has seldom been projected with such
excitement and power as Brown can command.

Arnold Shaw 1969 •54

None of the new generation can ever be the Godfather.
The only people that qualify are myself and Sinatra.
It's God's business that nobody can fill my shoes.

James Brown 1988 •55

This was my richest time, with all my hit records
selling all over the country and me and my
band working every night. The river was
running. The river of loot.

Little Richard •56

Smokey is lovely. He sings lead in the perfect woman's soprano, not a falsetto shriek or anything so vulgar, but a finely controlled warble, full of its own small subtleties. Pop's first female impersonator, original prima donna.

Nik Cohn on Smokey Robinson •57

Every time you hear his voice on the radio, you feel that they're playing music again.

Bobby Womack on Smokey Robinson •58

In person, everything he does is an all out, powerhouse, total emotional explosion. He may start singing *Try a Little Tenderness* with tenderness, but it always ends up 'sock it to me, baby...' he can work listeners into a frenzy more quickly than any nightclub performer of his time. *Ralph J. Gleason* on Otis Redding •59

Modulation, shading, dynamics, progression, emotion. Every essential quality — he had it all.

Jerry Wexler on Sam Cooke •60

You had to crossover — get the white business as well as the black business.

Curtis Mayfield •61

In the manner of the very greatest rock 'n' roll, Sly and the Family Stone made music no one had ever heard before.

Greil Marcus •62

Curtis Mayfield, for me, is an encyclopaedia. Every time I listen to his songs they never seem to age, and they always seem appropriate for whatever else is going on in society.

Jazzie B on the influential Curtis Mayfield •63

There's nobody in the world can make better records than I do.

Phil Spector •64

In the 1960s they all treated us like we were great philosopher gods that knew all the answers…

Paul Kantner of Jefferson Airplane •65

We were inspiring each other. I miss [the 1960's] quite a bit. I think about how great music was then and how inspired everybody was. It seems like it's all gone away. People aren't making very many records these days. *Brian Wilson* of The Beach Boys, 2001 •66

Never was it easier to gain
a reputation as a seer, never
was a following so rapidly
and readily acquired.

Bernard Levin on the Sixties,
The Pendulum Years, 1970 •67

Skiffle was the start of British rock music. It was
all about feel rather than content. It had style.

Lonnie Donegan •68

I strode onstage wearing an eye patch
after being struck in the eye by a guitar
string — and never looked back.

Johnny Kidd of Johnny Kidd and the Pirates •69

I'm not being big headed, but The Kinks were unique — it's like getting to the North Pole first. Really, until we started diversifying, we couldn't be touched.

The modest *Ray Davies* •70

When Lou and I started the group, there was a basic understanding: it seemed more important to be different than immediately successful, to have a personality of our own, to have arrangements like *Venus In Furs* and to give concerts that were never the same. *John Cale* on the Velvet Underground •71

I won't retire until the people retire me.

B.B. King •72

What rock needed to get it off the ground was
a universal hero, a symbol, a rallying point…
obviously, Bill Haley didn't measure up.
Equally obviously, Elvis Presley did…

Nik Cohn in Awopbopaloobop, 1968 •73

The reason I taped Elvis was this: over and over I remember
Sam saying, if only I could find a white man who had the Negro
feel, I could make a billion dollars. This is what I heard in Elvis, this.…
what I guess they now call soul, this Negro sound.

Marion Keisher who made the first taped recording of Elvis •74

This was the major teen breakthrough and Elvis
triggered it. In this way, without even trying, he
became one of the people who have radically
affected the way that people think and live.

Nik Cohn •75

The teddy boys were waiting for Elvis Presley.
Everybody under 20 all over the world was waiting.

Jeff Nuttall in Bomb Culture, 1968 •76

This was punk rock. This was revolt. It's all there in that elastic voice and body.

Bono on Elvis •77

If the police had not been there, forming a blue wall on the stage, the audience might have eaten Elvis's body in a Eucharistic frenzy. They were his and he was theirs, the leader: it was the incandescent moment.

Stanley Booth on Elvis' famous Memphis charity concert in 1956 •78

The story of Heartbreak Hotel is this: Mae Boren Axton, songwriter and Hank Snow's PR lady, was shown a newspaper clipping by her friend Tommy Durden, another songwriter. The clipping reported a suicide by a young man who left a one line note, 'I walk a lonely street'. Axton and Durden wrote the song around the line and made a tape of it within half an hour.

Nick Tosches •79

Blue Suede Shoes was even more to the point. This had been a hit for Carl Perkins in 1956 as Elvis took it over the following year and give it wholly new dimensions. It was important — the idea that clothes could dominate your life.
Nik Cohn 1968 •80

When I first met Elvis, he had a million dollars worth of talent. Now he has a million dollars.
Colonel Tom Parker •81

I don't aim to let this fame business get me. God gave me a voice. If I turned against God, I'd be finished.
Elvis Presley quoted by Tony Palmer, 1976 •82

The kind of stardom that was visited on Elvis Presley was simply more than he could handle.
Charles Shaar Murray •83

Elvis is the dream gone wrong, that's why
as a character he's so fascinating. His demise
was such a public one. He was for a lot of people
the definition of America, all its promise, all it
could achieve and all the freedom of the country.
The Edge •84

The awful spectacle of a great star,
falling apart among servants and
minders, shocked Elton to the core.
Philip Norman on Elton John's meeting with Elvis in 1976 •85

Elvis Presley is a supreme figure in American
life, one whose presence, no matter how banal
or predictable, brooks no real comparisons.
Greil Marcus in Mystery Train, 1977 •86

His violent hip-swinging during an
obvious attempt to copy Elvis Presley
was revolting. Hardly the kind of
performance any parent could
wish their child to witness.
NME in 1958 on that notorious rebel,
Cliff Richard •87

Elvis Presley recorded a song of mine…
that's the one recording I treasure the most…
it was called *Tomorrow Is A Long Time.*
Bob Dylan •88

I'm a really big Elvis fan and I think the reason why we did
the whole Elvis thing is because, you know, he's from Vegas.
Britney Spears •89

The book is a prodigy of bad writing,
excitable, sarcastic and only fleetingly
literate. It is also as exploitative as the
exploiters whom Goldman reviles, and
no more tasteful than an Elvis jumpsuit.
Martin Amis **on Albert Goldman's Elvis** •90

Mini tycoon Jonathan King, radiantly happy to be in front of
the cameras even on such a solemn occasion, said that this was
a doubly important death because the man doing the dying had
been entirely created by the media. Tony Palmer said it would be
a pity to leave the audience with the impression that anyone as
talented as Elvis Presley had been entirely created by the media.
Jonathan King said, 'I agree with Tony Palmer'.
Clive James **in The Observer, on a TV tribute to Elvis** •91

I tell you, Elvis can't last.

Jackie Gleason 1956 •92

Elvis is where pop begins and ends.
He's the great original and, even now,
he's the image that makes all others
seem shoddy; the boss. For once,
the fan club's spiel is justified:
Elvis is King.

Nik Cohn •93

If life was fair, Elvis would be alive and all the impersonators would be dead.

Johnny Carson The Tonight Show, NBC TV •94

When I first heard Elvis' voice I just knew
I wasn't going to work for anybody, and nobody
was going to be my boss. Hearing him for the
first time was like busting out of jail.

Bob Dylan •95

There have been contenders. There have been pretenders. But there is still only one King — Elvis Presley.

Bruce Springsteen 1975 •96

I think of a hero as someone who understands the degree of responsibility that comes with his freedom.

Bob Dylan, from the sleeve notes to Biograph (1985) •97

Louis Jordan's *Saturday Night Fish Fry* is the perfect
record. Somewhere between jump, jazz and R&B, it
is a whole way of life in one song — it shows that
rock and roll did not start with Bill Haley.
Jerry Dammers of The Specials •98

My music made your liver quiver, your bladder spatter, your knees freeze. And your big toe shoot right up in your boot.

Little Richard •99

He'd scream and scream and scream. He had a freak
voice, tireless, hysterical, completely indestructible,
and he never in his life sang at anything lower than
an enraged bull like roar. On every phrase, he'd
embroider with squeals, rasps, siren whoops.
His stamina, his drive were limitless.
Nik Cohn **on Little Richard** •100

46

You knew not, night to night, where he was going
to come from. He just burst onto the stage from
anywhere. You wouldn't be able to hear anything but
the roar of the audience. He might come out and walk
on the piano. He might go out into the audience. His
charisma was just a whole new thing to the business.
Richard was totally out of this world, wild, and it gave
people who wanted to scream a chance to go ahead
and scream instead of trying to be cool.

H.B.Barnum **Richard's sax player** •101

As a person he was brash, fast, bombastic, a sort of prototype Muhammad Ali.

Nik Cohn **on Little Richard** •102

He drove the whole house into a complete frenzy.
There is no single phrase to describe his hold on
the audience. It might excite some and terrify others.
It's hypnotic, like an evangelistic meeting where,
for want of a better phrase, Richard is the disciple and
the audience the flock that follows. I couldn't believe
the power of Little Richard on stage. He was amazing.

Mick Jagger •103

Jerry Lee learned how to rock 'n' roll from me.
He was just a country singer till he heard my
songs and he recorded a lot of them.
Little Richard on his influence on Jerry Lee Lewis •104

Richard taught Hendrix a lot of things, and
Hendrix got a lot of things from Richard. That's
where he got the charisma. Richard used to say,
look, don't be ashamed to do whatever you feel.
Marquette Little Richard's road manager •105

They asked me to come back the next day
and I said if they gave me ten bob I would.
So they gave me the ten bob and I came back.
Noël Redding on joining Jimi Hendrix' band •106

James Brown and Frank Sinatra are two different quantities in the universe. They represent two different experiences of the world.

Amiri Baraka poet and activist, in an interview with David Frost 1970 •107

If you're talking about really
heavy people — heavy, heavy,
heavy — I'd say Burt Bacharach.

James Brown •108

Michael Jackson, he used to watch me from
the wings and got his moon walk from my
camel walk. I ain't jealous, I'm zealous.
I ain't teased, I'm pleased.

James Brown •109

I've always loved Steve Winwood. I used to go and see the
Spencer Davis Group when I was 18 and he was about 16.
He used to play really great guitar as well as great piano
— I wanted to hit the little fucker, he was so good!

Dave Gilmour of Pink Floyd •110

A perfect record from start to finish
— you couldn't improve on it.

George Harrison on Tina Turner's River Deep, Mountain High,
masterfully produced by Phil Spector •111

Stylistically, I've always said that we can't be a heavy riff group because Led Zeppelin are the best in the world. We can't be a blues influenced R&B rock 'n' roll group because The Stones are the best in the world. We can't be a slightly sort of airy-fairy mystical synthesizing abstract freak-out group because Pink Floyd are the best in the world. And so what's left? And that's what we've always done. We've filled the gap. We've done what's left.

Ian Anderson explains Jethro Tull's niche •112

His tone is vocal; his ideas are superb; he plays almost exclusively blues — all the lines he plays in Cream are blues lines. He's a blues guitarist and he's taken blues guitar to its ultimate thing.

Mike Bloomfield on Eric Clapton •113

I always loved Roy. I looked up to the way he was, admired the way he handled himself. That aloofness he had influenced me profoundly.

Neil Young on Roy Orbison, 1990 •114

I wanted to make a record that would sound like Phil Spector. I wanted to write words like Dylan. I wanted my guitar to sound like Duane Eddy.

Bruce Springsteen 1987 •115

I should be sending Pete Townshend cards for Fathers' Day.

Eddie Vedder of Pearl Jam, 1995 •116

Since *New Boots and Panties* became the working man's *Tubular Bells*, Ian Dury has been adopted as some sort of mascot, as treasured and beloved an emblem as a battered teddy bear with a ripped ear and scorch marks on its fur.

Charles Shaar Murray 1979 •117

The Sex Pistols got it right, man; they made a good record, then blew up. I love that.

Chris Balew of The Presidents of the United States of America, 2000 •118

There's a real melancholy in [Abba's] songs…
all the flourishes, like big double octaves on
the piano, we stole them like crazy.

Elvis Costello 1991 •119

I was on holiday and passed an amusement
arcade where it was playing on the jukebox.
There was a magic to it that made me want
to be a part of the world it came from.

Bob Harris on how Paul Anka's Diana encouraged
him to embrace rock and roll •120

When I was a teenager, I loved The Buzzcocks,
Generation X, Elvis Costello, If you look at what
those artists sold, they weren't selling big in
a world full of hack artists that were selling
millions and millions of records.

Matthew Sweet 2001 •121

My access to music when I was growing up was through pirate radio,
you know, transistor radio under the pillow, listening to one more
and then 'just one more' until your favourite track comes on.

Robert Palmer •122

When The Smiths came on Top Of The Pops for the first time, that was it for me. From that day on I wanted to be Johnny Marr. *Noel Gallagher* **of Oasis, 2000** •123

I get that tingle when I listen to Joy Division or The Smiths. There was something really weird going on with those bands, they created their own rules and life and aura. *Jimi Goodwin* **of Doves, 2000** •124

If I were knocked down tomorrow by a passing train, I would be considered the most important artist ever in the history of English pop music. That's just a rough guess. *Morrissey* **in typically mischievous mood in a 1991 interview** •125

When I saw The Stone Roses, I thought I could do that. And I did, didn't I?

Noel Gallagher **of Oasis, 1994.** •126

The first band I ever felt a part of were The Jam.
I was a teenager and they were the best group in
England. Paul Weller was the coolest pop singer.
Totally. The Jam always had a single out every three
months, which is what Oasis are trying to emulate.

Noel Gallagher 1994 •127

Even if I were talentless, after seeing
Echo and The Bunnymen eight million
times and Nirvana ten million times, how
could I not write an okay new wave record?

Courtney Love of Hole, 1994 •128

Rob, top five musical crimes perpetuated
by Stevie Wonder in the 80s and 90s. Go.
Sub-question: is it in fact unfair to criticize
a formerly great artist for his latter day sins,
is it better to burn out or fade away?

Jack Black as Barry interrogating his boss
(John Cusack) in High Fidelity (2000) •129

I read these interviews with him and I don't know who the guy is who's in these interviews, he seems really cool, because the guy I've been in a band with for the last eighteen years is a fucking nobhead.

Noel Gallagher on younger brother, Liam, clearly NOT one of his heroes •130

I have this huge catalogue of melodies in my head, and I've heard it all, the Merseybeat thing, late 60s psychedelic, glam rock, prog rock. I was there for it all. So that's all part of me. 'Guided by Voices' name refers to all those influences. That's what the voices are. *Bob Pollard* of Guided By Voices, 2001 •131

I met Coldplay, and they were nice guys, But then I heard *Yellow* and thought 'Oh, that's a big song That's a huge song

Fran Healy of Travis, 2001 •132

Homer Simpson: You know, my kids think you're the greatest. And thanks to your gloomy music, they've finally stopped dreaming of a future I can't possibly provide.

Billy Corgan: Well, we try to make a difference.

The Smashing Pumpkins frontman does a good deed •133

We don't think The Beatles will do anything in this market.

Head of Capitol records, *Jay Livingstone* in 1964 •134

There in the centre tunnel on a raised platform was
a sight that galvanised him. It was in the most specific
way a personification of his secret sexual desires. On
stage were four young men dressed in leather trousers
and jackets. They played good time rock and roll and
joked with each other with macho camaraderie.

Peter Brown describes Brian Epstein's first visit to the Cavern Club in 1961 •135

I'm all for perfection as long as it doesn't take
more than eight weeks because then it's a bore.

John Lennon 1974 •136

I wanted to manage those four
boys. It wouldn't take me more
than two half days a week.

Brian Epstein in 1961, after seeing The Beatles •137

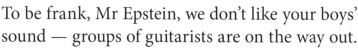

To be frank, Mr Epstein, we don't like your boys'
sound — groups of guitarists are on the way out.

Head of Decca records, *Dick Rowe* in 1962 •138

By the end of 1963, Brian Epstein was able to look back at a year in
which his artists had dominated the hit parade with an incredible nine
number ones, spanning 32 weeks at the top. No manager in British pop
history has ever achieved comparable chart supremacy.

Johnny Rogan **1988 •139**

We were all on this ship in the sixties, our generation,
a ship going to discover the New World. And
The Beatles were in the crow's nest of that ship.

John Lennon **1974, quoted in Imagine, 1988 •140**

They are, in my mind, responsible for most
of the degeneration that has happened, not
only musically but also in the sense of
youth orientation and politically, too. They
are the people who made it first publicly
acceptable to spit in the eye of authority.

Frank Sinatra **on The Beatles •141**

Rock and roll isn't a form of entertainment. It's a culture, a civilisation. It has taken over the past half-century. There's never been anything like it. And here is a man who was one of the greatest masters of it, who embodies its essence. Aren't we going to learn something about this whole civilisation if we look at its leaders?

Albert Goldman on John Lennon •142

The very first tune I ever learned to play was *That'll Be the Day*. My mother taught me to play it on the banjo, sitting there with endless patience until I managed to work out all the chords.

John Lennon •143

One gets the impression they think simultaneously of harmony and melody, so firmly are the major tonic sevenths and ninths built into their tunes.

Walter Mann on Lennon & McCartney's songs in The Times,1963 •144

I discovered the frabjous falsetto shriek-cum-croon, the ineluctable beat, the flawless intonation, the utterly fresh lyrics, the Schubert-like flow of musical invention, and the fuck-you coolness of these Four Horsemen of Our Apocalypse.

Leonard Bernstein 1979 •145

It is possible to see in The Beatles' music a synthesis in which one of the strongest elements has been a powerful and probably instinctive Englishry… which goes back… to pastoral pentatonic tunes and other revitalised archaisms.
The Times leader column, 1967 •146

> Rock 'n' roll is the music that inspired me to play music. There is nothing conceptually better than rock 'n' roll. No group, be it the Beatles, Dylan or the Stones have ever improved on *Whole Lotta Shakin'* for my money. Or maybe, like our parents, that's my period and I'll dig it and never leave it. *John Lennon* •147

The 12 songs on *Sgt. Pepper* set a new standard of achievement in popular music. It took only four months to record, at a cost of £100,000. It was so different and stunning to hear at first that when The Beach Boys' Brian Wilson first listened to it, he gave up work on his own forthcoming album, thinking that the quintessential album had already been made. *Peter Brown* •148

> Oh, I get it. You don't want to be cute any more.
> *Bob Dylan's* reaction to Sgt. Pepper's •149

That's what this new record, The White Album, is about. Definitely rocking. What we were doing on Pepper was rocking, and not rocking.
John Lennon on The White Album •150

Forgive the Beatles; they just didn't know any better. How could they? What happened to them had not happened to anybody else before except Elvis, and look what happened to him. *Charles Shaar Murray* •151

Reporter: Would you like to walk down the street without being recognised?
Lennon: We used to do that with no money in our pockets. There's no point to it.
John Lennon 1964 •152

Big bastards, that's what The Beatles were. You have to be a bastard to make it. And The Beatles were the biggest bastards on earth. *John Lennon* 1980 •153

We're kidding you, we're kidding ourselves, we're kidding everybody. We don't take anything seriously except the money. *John Lennon* •154

There are a staggering number of similarities between Lennon and Elvis. The two greatest men in the history of rock 'n' roll, which is how I conceive of Elvis and Lennon… are both momma's boys. They were very bluesy, melancholic, withdrawn people looking for powerful, dominating keepers to direct them and also protect them. Both drifting off into the world of drugs. Both taken up with fantasies of being Jesus, of coming back as the messiah, and all that. Very unfulfilled by their fame. *Albert Goldman* 1988 •155

Christianity will go. It will vanish and shrink. I needn't argue about that. I'm right and I'll be proved right. We're more popular than Jesus now.

John Lennon 1966 •156

Politics was one of John's ways of struggling with being rich. In a sense, to John, being rich was selling out. He was by instinct part socialist, part right-wing Archie Bunker; to be an indolent, wealthy rock star would have made him feel as guilty as sin.

Peter Brown •157

My defences were so great. The cocky rock and roll hero who knows all the answers was actually a terrified guy who didn't know how to cry. Simple.

John Lennon Playboy 1980 •158

Lots of people who complained about us receiving the MBE received theirs for heroism in the war — for killing people. We received ours for entertaining other people. I'd say we deserve ours more.

John Lennon 1969 •159

On this trip John managed to surpass his previous craziness. One night he walked on stage naked with a toilet seat around his neck to the cheers of the audience.

Peter Brown on The Beatles' performances in Hamburg in 1961 •160

John Lennon had a profound intolerance of children, being too much of a child himself to tolerate any rivals

Albert Goldman •161

I didn't blame John or Yoko. I understood their love. I knew there was no way I could ever fight the unity of mind and body that they had with each other. *Cynthia Lennon* •162

I like that first John Lennon album a hell of a lot. I think all
the songs are really beautifully written and very straight
from the shoulder. There's an honesty in the lyrics there.

David Bowie •163

I'm a smoke-screen expert. I lie all the time. It is the price of fame.

Paul McCartney The Observer 1998 •164

McCartney is one of those people who everyone's
got too much attitude about. If you see how many
lives pop music has destroyed from a fleeting
moment's fame, its kinda remarkable that he's
still so fluent. People forget what a good musician
the guy is, what a great rock 'n' roll singer.

Elvis Costello 1989 •165

We'll never get to that stage of releasing rubbish because we know people will buy it.

Paul McCartney 1965. Frog Chorus anyone? •166

I've never really done anything to create what has happened. It creates itself. I'm here because it happened. But I didn't do anything to make it happen other than saying 'Yes'.

Ringo Starr •167

Does Ringo exist apart from his records? Who cares? It's doubtful the cutesy-pie tracks Richard Perry has turned into Ringo Records will ever move a listener to do anything more than reach for the radio dial and that's what's so unnerving about these records. These cuts — this *No No Song*, that thoughtless remake of *Only You, Oh My My, You're Sixteen* — they're maddening only for their lack of personality, depth, emotional commitment. They're so insubstantial they're hardly fit objects to provoke boredom, much less concern and despair.

Gene Sculatti March 1976 •168

I'm just a dog and I'm led around by my collar by Krishna.

George Harrison •169

After the spiritual life with George,
within a few weeks of going to live
with Eric I seemed to be surrounded
by mayhem. I drank like a fish too.

Patti Harrison on life in the Clapton household •170

To be fair, the movie does show a certain charm in its
relentlessly stupid grasp of the obvious. When Frampton
sings *The Long and Winding Road*, for example, he is
walking down a long and winding road. You keep
laughing and thinking it can't get any worse. But it does.

Charles M. Young on Beatles movie Sgt. Pepper's Lonely Hearts Club
Band, in Rolling Stone magazine, 1978 •171

His place in history was already reserved as the most
luckless of all might-have-beens. In the next 24 months,
The Beatles would gross £17 million. Pete Best became
a banker, earning £8 a week, and married a girl named
Kathy who worked at the biscuit counter at Woolworth's.

Peter Brown •172

Was I the fifth Beatle? Not really.

George Best •173

I've met them.
Delightful lads.
Absolutely
no talent.

Noël Coward •174

You put a greased, naked woman on all fours, with a dog collar around her neck, and a leash, and the man's arm extended out up to here, holding on to the leash and pushing a black glove in her face to sniff it. You don't find that offensive?

Fran Deschler as Bobbi, debating Spinal Tap's new album cover (This Is Spinal Tap) (1984) •175

We were the first band ever to have big 4 x 12 cabinets. I was the first bass player to have two stacks, the first bass player to have two amps. We were the first really loud group.

John Entwistle of The Who 1974 •176

If you take everything in the universe and break it down to a common denominator, all you've got is energy. That's the essence of the urban sound.

Wayne Kramer of MC5s •177

Jimmy Page represented all that was ethereal, exquisite, divine, and pornographic in rock music...

Pamela Des Barres on the Led Zeppelin guitarist, 1989 •178

I wanted to be in a band that gave bang for the buck. I wanted to be in the band who didn't look like a bunch of guys who, you know, should be in a library studying for their finals.

Gene Simmons **of Kiss •179**

Fifty per cent of the things you hear about Alice Cooper is urban legend. But everything you hear about Keith Moon is true and you've only heard ten per cent of it. Every day was an event with Keith.

Alice Cooper on the legendary Who drummer •180

I remember arguing with him once, after a few whiskeys… next thing I know, I got my teeth knocked out. That's how he led the band.

Lynyrd Skynyrd's *Billy Powell* **on Steve Van Zandt's leadership technique •181**

It's just rock and roll. A lot of times we get criticised for it. A lot of music papers come out with: 'When are they going to stop playing these three chords?' If you believe you shouldn't play just three chords it's pretty silly on their part. To us, the simpler a song is, the better, 'cause it's more in line with what the person on the street is.

Angus Young **of AC/DC in the Atlanta Gazette, 1980 •182**

AC/DC's *Highway to Hell* is the greatest meshing of vocal, guitar and content I've ever heard. That's what I aspire to.

Bonnie Raitt 2000 •183

If it was happening, I'd call it Heavenly Beast. If it wasn't happening, I usually call it Asshole.

Angus Young in Rolling Stone,on being asked if his guitar had a name •184

Cooper is a master charlatan; indeed, he has elevated charlatanry to a higher artistic plane than anybody else in rock and roll had ever dreamed of.

Charles Shaar Murray on Alice Cooper •185

Fuck Elvis and Keith Richards! Lemmy's the king of
rock 'n' roll. He's a living, breathing, drinking and
snorting fucking legend. No one else comes close.
Foo Fighters' *Dave Grohl* **on Lemmy, 2006** •186

I took *Spinal Tap* real personal. I was really high at the time
and Aerosmith was sinking — we were like a boat going
down. And that movie was way too close, way too real.
Steven Tyler **of Aerosmith, 1990** •187

There are things I don't remember. I'd wake up
with bumps on my head, blood on my shirt and
something green coming out of my penis.
Iggy Pop **on his wild years** •188

It's almost like we'd get worried if
we got a good review. My daughter's
homework reports are better than
our reviews. *Steve Harris* **of Iron Maiden** •189

Whoever you name, Dave Lee Roth was undoubtedly
the most over-the-top, larger-than-life rock star you
could ever hope to meet. *Mick Wall* **on Van Halen's main man** •190

Metallica is just four lucky friends that got together and started playing… this could be you!

James Hetfield of Metallica •191

"If you came here to see spandex, eye makeup, and the words 'Ooh baby' in every fuckin' song, this ain't the fuckin' band. We came to bang some heads."

Jaymz Hetfield, of Metallica in 1985 •192

Bon Jovi are a kind of simpleton's version of heavy rock. Their messages, about love, friendship or life on the road, are big and generalised. Corny, even.

Adam Sweeting •193

We're like a fuckin' grenade and it's like everybody's struggling to hold the pin in!

Slash of Guns N' Roses, 1988 •194

I don't care if you think I'm being big-headed. This is the only rock'n'roll band to come out of LA that's real.

Slash •195

It's just such cool chemistry between us. We've been together for so long and care about each other so much, it's really like brothers.

Adam Yauch of Beastie Boys, 1998 •196

The first thing I remember of Pearl Jam was hearing *'Alive'* on the radio while I was living in Seattle. I pictured Mountain or some serious '70s throwback. The music just seemed like classic rock to me, so I pictured the singer being some husky, fuckin' bearded, leather-jacketed Tad type. Big and fat and tortured and scary. *Dave Grohl* of Nirvana and The Foo Fighters, 2001 •197

This hi-wattage trio doesn't seem to belong to Geffen, but this is combative, heavy-hitting rock that thinks on its feet. Slightly Pixies-like, but less whimsical. Big in '92. *Adam Sweeting* on the release of Nevermind in 1991. Clever boy. •198

Nirvana slayed the hair bands. They shot the top off the poodles. All of a sudden, all those bands like Poison, Bon Jovi and Warrant became like Rommel in the desert: overextended, bloated, no more Vaseline. And now they're just rusty tanks in the desert with no gas. Nirvana is going to be remembered for changing the face of rock.
Henry Rollins 1994 •199

> Don't talk to me about Nirvana. He was a sad man who couldn't handle the fame. We're stronger than that. And you can fuck your fucking Pearl Jam. *Liam Gallagher* sensitive soul, 1994 •200

It wasn't always comfortable competing against Nirvana, and it was certainly not healthy living under that shadow at times. But at least there was honour in it. We all respected that it was a great band — Pearl Jam too. But competing against Bush? It's nothing to get your dick hard about, you know what I mean? There's no mojo in that!
Billy Gallagher of The Smashing Pumpkins, 1996 •201

I know nothing about rock and roll. Do you know, until recently I thought that Led Zeppelin sang *Smoke On The Water*?
Justine Frischmann of Elastica, 1994 •202

I guess it's like folk music, only really loud.

Gary Louris of The Jayhawks describing his band's sound, 1995 •203

It's basically angry bubblegum.

Dave Wyndorf of Monster Magnet, 2001 •204

I started rapping because I couldn't fucking sing.

Coby Dick of Papa Roach, 2000 •205

You're seeing black people at metal shows
and white people at hip-hop shows.
Everything's starting to melt together.

Fred Durst of Limp Bizkit •206

You wonder why we sound the way
we do? We were born in scum, we
live in filth and we die in dirt.

Max Cavalera of Sepultura •207

I turn on the TV and there's this band, tattoos, shirts off…
I laugh at first, but then I get kind of sad. People really
think this is the alternative. It's a bunch of millionaires
pretending to be bad boys, pretending to be pivotal
components of youth. *John Reis* of Rocket From The Crypt, 2001 •208

I'm just a regular guy, you know?
There's no leotard and cape under my
clothes. I shit, I piss, I drink too much
and throw up, just like everybody else.

Chester Bennington of Linkin Park, 2001 •209

This tragic bombardment of tuneless metal cliché fails
to move in any direction other than towards the bin.

Steve Beebee on Debase's album Domination, in Kerrang, October 2001 •210

Macho rap-rock from the UK. Horrible, horrible.
This is the sound of five men in competition to
prove who has the most testosterone.

Emma Johnston on nu-metal band Lillydamnwhite's
album Eviscerate in Kerrang, July 2001 •211

The still-born brainchild of Korn bassist Reginald Fieldy Arvizu, *Rock 'n' Roll Gangster* is an utterly unlikeable gangsta-rap pastiche. When not tiresomely trumpeting his titanic weed intake, Fieldy stumbles through sterilised sex rhymes and banal B-boy bragging so devoid of charm or wit that they make the similarly salacious Kid Rock sound like Stephen Fry in comparison.

Dan Silver on the album Rock 'n' Roll Gangster by Fieldy's Dreams, in Q magazine, January 2002 •212

Three tracks in this truly lamentable opus and you'll have lost the will to live; four tracks and you'll be weeping openly into your coffee cup.

James Cooper on heavy metal band Solstice's album Lamentations in Kerrang, August 2001 •213

All rock musicians are deaf...
Or insensitive to mellow sounds.

Marc Bolan •214

Of all the things I've lost, it's my mind I miss the most.

Ozzy Osbourne •215

…the combo they writhe and twist to is called The Rolling Stones.
Maybe you've never heard of them — if you live far from London,
the odds are you haven't. But, by gad, you will!
**Norman Jopling of the Record Mirror reviews
the Stones' 1962 gig at the Crawdaddy** •216

For most people, the fantasy is driving around in a big car, having
all the chicks you want and being able to pay for it. It always has been,
still is, and always will be. And anyone who says it isn't is talking bullshit.
Mick Jagger •217

Mick Jagger is the greatest performer since Nijinsky.

Patti Smith •218

He moves like a parody between a majorette girl and Fred Astaire.

Truman Capote on Mick Jagger •219

I think rock 'n' roll is all frivolity — it should
be about pink satin suits and white socks.

Mick Jagger •220

Mick Jagger is the perfect pop star. There's nobody more perfect than Jagger. He is rude, he's ugly-attractive, he's brilliant. The Rolling Stones are the perfect pop group — they don't give a shit. *Elton John* •221

> I wanted to be an actress, and a scholar too. My first move was to get a Rolling Stone as a boyfriend. I slept with three, then decided that the singer was the best.
>
> *Marianne Faithfull* •222

Rock and roll is the rhythm of our generation. It is the epitome of the kind of rhythm our generation grew up with, it is very natural to them. As long as this generation carries on, rock 'n' roll will live with it. But now there's a new generation and it's searching for its own rhythm. Each generation has its own rhythm. Our parents had swing, we had rock and the kids of today are taking our stuff and interpreting it for their time and for their feeling of life.

Keith Richards 1991 •223

I never liked *Revolver* very much. I don't like the Beatles. I'm not saying that I never liked anything they did and I'm not saying that they didn't influence me, because it's impossible not to be influenced by them. *Mick Jagger* 1974 •224

The Rolling Stones. It took the people from England to hip my people — my white people — to what they had in their own backyard. That sounds funny, but it's the truth.
Muddy Waters •225

In 1963, Andrew Loog Oldham became The Rolling Stones' manager. Oldham, without doubt, was the most flash personality that British pop has ever had, the most anarchic and obsessive and imaginative hustler of all. Whenever he was good, he was quite magnificent. *Nik Cohn* •226

Actually, if you're a musician I think it's very good not to be with anybody and just live on your own. Domesticity is death.

Mick Jagger 1974 •227

Narcissism and arrogance, concisely set out in *Get off My Cloud*, are the keynote of most of The Stones' lyrics.

Alan Beckett in New Left Review, 1967 •228

Mick's an old friend of mine. Our battles aren't exactly what people think they are. There are many different levels — it's not just 'who runs The Rolling Stones?' *Keith Richards* 1988 •229

I don't want audiences to be in awe.
I just want them to have a good time.
With Woody, the band is more good-timey.

Mick Jagger on bandmate Ronnie Wood, 1976 •230

I'm sick of playing places like Madison Square Garden. I want to play some small towns. I'm sick of playing places where everyone in the audience looks as good, or better, than I do. *Keith Richards* 1973 •231

I've been asked if this is the last tour since I was 19 years old.

Mick Jagger •232

Let it be acknowledged: there are very few performers in the world who could dominate a vast audience of 20,000 as he did. Narcissist, freak, dandy, dancer, rocker, God, devil, stripper, sensualist, tease — the women in the audience are not there for the popcorn — Mr Jagger at 38 is still a kind of wild animal. His athleticism, the result of jogging several miles a day, is phenomenal. He has become the Nureyev of rock 'n' roll.

**John Heilpern on The Rolling Stones
at Madison Square Garden in 1981** •233

I'd rather be dead than singing *Satisfaction* when I'm 45.

Mick Jagger **45, no way, but 61 is cool** •234

At the Grammy Awards, Keith Richards became the first performer ever to accept a posthumous award in Britain.

Jay Leno The Tonight Show, NBC •235

It's like a monkey with arthritis trying to go on stage and look young.

Elton John on Keith Richards, 1997 •236

I heard Muddy Waters play six months before he died and he was as powerful and strong as ever. So I say, good, let's find out. It's an uncharted area now for a rock 'n' roll band to go on this far. I'm looking forward to it — there's a sort of Columbus feel about it.

Keith Richards 1991 •237

I hope to be half as cool as The Stones for half as long.

Jon Bon Jovi 1989 •238

It's all right letting your self go, as long as you can get your self back.

Mick Jagger •239

I asked a ouija board once if I'd ever be in a rock band. It said no, and I was crushed.

Fred Schneider of The B-52's •240

One of the things which has impressed me most in life was the Mod movement in England, which was an incredible youthful thing. It was a movement of young people, much bigger than the hippy thing, the underground and all these things. It was an army, a powerful, aggressive army of teenagers with transport.

Pete Townshend •241

That's all I wanted to do as a kid. Play a guitar properly and jump around.

Syd Barrett 1971 •242

To the outside adult eye, Punk Rock is the weirdest, ugliest, nastiest, scariest, most thoroughly repulsive and flat-out incomprehensible variant on the Teenage Wasteland formula that they've ever seen.

Charles Shaar Murray 1977 •243

At its best New Wave/punk represents a fundamental and age-old Utopian dream: that if you give people the license to be as outrageous as they want in absolutely any fashion they can dream up, they'll be creative about it, and do something good besides.

Lester Bangs in NME, 1977 •244

Some people have wives and girlfriends.
I had the New York Dolls.

Morrissey quoted in Mojo 2006 •245

The Ramones are pocket punks, a perfect razor edged bubblegum band. They should never make an album. They should make a single every week, 'cos they've already got enough songs to last them for the first six months.

Charles Shaar Murray in the NME 1975 •246

Nobody's gonna like you guys, but I'll have you back.

Hilly Kristal owner of CBGB, to The Ramones
after their first audition 1974 •247

If it wasn't for The Ramones, or Joey in particular, there wouldn't be a Green Day, an Offspring, a Rancid, a Blink 182 — there wouldn't be any punk band, period. There are bands that are influenced by The Ramones that don't even know it yet.

Billie Joe Armstrong of Green Day, 2001 •248

Androgynously, sullenly, sculpturally gorgeous, she had the air of a young Keith Richards about to embark on an evening's debauchery. It's still the only album I've ever bought for its sleeve.

Joseph O'Connor on Patti Smith's Horses •249

Horses tore my limbs off and put them back in a whole different order.

Michael Stipe on Patti Smith's influential 1975 album. We think he liked it. •250

They were musically, culturally, in every way, the best thing in the world.

Tony Wilson on The Sex Pistols •251

No one in this band is a musician. We all
hate the term. We're something close to
factory-workers. Machinists. Skilled operators.
John Lydon (as Johnny Rotten), quoted
in Rock'n'Roll Babylon, 1982 •252

Who the fuck wrote the rules about music? Why are we following
this slavish idiocy? That was the difference between me and
Glen Matlock. He thought music ended when Chuck Berry
declared that rock 'n' roll was four to the bar. For me, it's
twenty-two of my mates AT the bar. *John Lydon* •253

Punks in their silly leather jackets are a cliché.
I never liked the term and have never discussed it.
I just got on with it and got out of it when it became
a competition. *John Lydon* The Observer, 1986 •254

I don't have to be pretentious or fake to
impress anyone around me because they all
know exactly what I am. A big fake cunt.
John Lydon of Public Image Ltd. 1998 •255

It wasn't like, 'These guys are great!' the thought was, 'Fuckin' A! if these
wankers can make music, we can make music.' Thing was, The Sex Pistols
were funny. Punks knew they looked ridiculous.
Bernard Sumner of New Order, 1993 •256

Ziggy Stardust had a mutant bastard offspring and his name was Johnny Rotten. *David Bowie* 1980 •257

Rock 'n' Roll is shit and it has to be cancelled. It's vile. It's dismal. A granddad dance.

John Lydon, PIL years, 1980 •258

Richard Branson doesn't even invite me round his house no more. That's because I usually beg for money and I hate cricket.

John Lydon •259

When I was about 14, I saw The Clash. I was pushed up close and people were stage-diving, and there was this sort of glorious, happy, violent chaos at work. It was like an indoctrination to the pain of the pit. I guess I was a little bit afraid, but I was also like, 'Well, actually, bring it; I like my bruises.' It was a sweet kind of pain.

Stephan Jenkins of Third Eye Blind, 2001 •260

We weren't misogynistic.
We were misanthropic.

Jean-Jacques Burnel of The Stranglers •261

My earliest memory is pretending to be dead. My mum used to step over me while I was laying on the kitchen floor.

Siouxsie Sioux of Siouxsie and The Banshees, 1993 •262

Mostly, punk was funny. We couldn't believe we were getting away with it.

Peter Shelley of The Buzzcocks, 2001 •263

I hated most of the punk bands. There was only
The Pistols and The Clash that I really liked. I thought
the rest were fucking rubbish. It's all right getting all
dewy-eyed and nostalgic, but it was fucking awful.
Paul Weller ex- The Jam, 1994 •264

We were the dustmen of punk.

Jimmy Pursey of Sham 69 •265

I try to talk in tune. That's what I do, talk in tune.

John Cooper Clarke •266

The thing about The Cure is that we exist in isolation.
We're not in competition with anyone. One day I
suppose we'll stop. But we'll never be replaced.
Robert Smith 1989 •267

I wish I could have taken a class on becoming a Rock Star. It might have prepared me for this. *Kurt Cobain* •268

My generation's apathy, I'm disgusted with it. I'm disgusted with my own apathy too, for being spineless and not always standing up against racism, sexism and all those other — isms the counterculture has been whining about for years.
Kurt Cobain •269

Punk is musical freedom. It's saying, doing and playing what you want. In Webster's terms, 'nirvana' means freedom from pain, suffering and the external world, and that's pretty close to my definition of Punk Rock.
Kurt Cobain •270

What people have got to understand is that we
are lads. We have burgled houses and nicked
car stereos, and we like girls and we swear
and we go to the football and we take the piss.
Noel Gallagher **prompting a police investigation
into banal utterances in 1996** •271

There has to be danger, we have to instil a sense
of fear in the audience and in ourselves.
Trent Reznor **of Nine Inch Nails** •272

I don't think what I do is original at all. It's
more out of faithfulness to my adolescent
dreams that I'm still doing this.
Rivers Cuomo **of Weezer, 2000** •273

I grew up as a rebellious kid who was always locked
up in his room. When I got out, I wasn't bad — I
just didn't know what was right or wrong.
Fred Durst **of Limp Bizkit, 1999** •274

We're not your average American band. We're not shit heads.
Mike Dirnt **of Green Day** •275

I think it's your own choice if you turn from an angry young man
to a bitter, old bastard, or if you stay hungry in a good way.
Billie Joe Armstrong **of Green Day, 2000** •276

We're not a political band and we don't want
to tell people what to do or what to think.
Billie Joe Armstrong **1997** •277

If I could see one band that I never got to see, it would be
Stiff Little Fingers. They were one of the first punk rock
bands I ever heard, and they're partially responsible for me
even playing guitar. *Tom DeLonge* **of Blink 182, 2001** •278

I guess it's all just music the way I look at it. It's hard to
call it rock & roll anymore… I think rock & roll is dead.
Billie Joe Armstrong **1995** •279

We made it easy for them to come and nick things
from us. They're sticky tape on a duck's arse.
John Lydon **questions Green Day's originality** •280

My mom used to tell me when I was a kid, 'If you curse at night-time, the devil's going to come to you when you're sleeping.' I used to get excited because I really wanted it to happen… I wanted it more than anything.

Marilyn Manson 1998 •281

Marilyn Manson is like a train wreck or a long form of suicide and people live vicariously through it. Sometimes I do things a lot of people wish they could do. If they don't wish they could do it, they enjoy being amused by it or being disgusted by it.

Marilyn Manson 1998 •282

He's ruthless, Machiavellian and great fun to be around. Humour isn't something that's normally associated with Marilyn Manson, but he's got an extremely dry wit.

Brian Molko of Placebo, 2000 •283

Eminem, he's good. Intense — intense and committed. He's got a lot to say and he says it. Vehemently.

Bruce Springsteen 2003 •284

I'm just a regular motherfucker. I'm Marshal Mathers before I'm Slim Shady, before I'm Eminem, before I'm anybody. *Eminem* 2000 •285

Slim Shady is just another part of me, the dark, evil, creatively sick part.

Eminem •286

God sent me to piss off the world.

Eminem 2000 •287

Musicians who didn't pay attention to punk have a gap in their knowledge that makes it difficult to communicate in this day and age.

Flea of The Red Hot Chili Peppers, 1992 •288

Being punk rock is not having to prove you are. It's obvious to anyone who is authentic in that mindset. You don't have to call yourself a punk rocker.

Thurston Moore of Sonic Youth 1994 •289

Country music is completely punk-rock. It's the original punk-rock.

Neko Case •290

Don't you think it's about time I grew up? I'm 43-years old, man.

Bob Pollard of Guided By Voices, 2001 •291

It's really sad that rock, especially alternative rock, has become corporate business.

Billy Corgan of The Smashing Pumpkins 1995 •292

I have this feeling record companies used to have more music lovers working for them. Rather than all bankers the way it is now — mostly bankers.

Evan Dando of The Lemonheads 1996 •293

What pisses me off is when I've got seven or eight record company fat pig men sitting there telling me what to wear.

Sinead O'Connor 1997 •294

I like the music business because as horrible an empire as it is and as tacky as it is, it's always in transition. They try to control things as much as they can but they can't — as much as they race around after it. And I like watching that because it's a real microcosm of society. You can't really control it. The safest thing is just to be aware of what is going on.

Thurston Moore of Sonic Youth, circa 1995 •295

In England everybody is trying to
make money but they're ashamed to
admit it. Here it's easy to talk business.

Jon Moss of Culture Club finds New York more to his taste •296

Music is spiritual.
The music business is not.

Van Morrison The Times, 1990 •297

Most bands don't make money. They just
squander it on producers and cocaine and lots
of other bullshit, and it's disgusting. There's so
much idiotic excess. It goes beyond enjoyment.

Sting •298

Rock never managed to die before it got old.
Instead, it put on a bit of weight and became
part of the showbusiness mainstream.

Adam Sweeting 1986 •299

There are two kinds of artists left; those who
endorse Pepsi and those who simply won't.

Annie Lennox 1990 •300

I hate the industry even more now, no bands get nurtured anymore. Labels only spend money promoting acts they know will be Top Ten. I find it offensive spending $2 million on a video.

Siouxsie Sioux •301

It's a radical time for musicians, a really revolutionary time, and I believe revolutions are a lot more fun than cash, which by the way we don't have at major labels anyway, so we might as well get with it and get in the game. *Courtney Love.* •302

What the major companies have done in the last few years is find out that they couldn't find any more Whitesnakes. They took a look at their marketing budget and put it behind hip-hop and figured out how to make it pop. *Chuck D* •303

The rock music business is a cruel and shallow trench, a long plastic hallway where thieves and pimps run free, and good men die like dogs. There is also a negative side.

Hunter S Thompson •304

He would bring me into his office and play me 16 different test pressings that only dogs could hear the differences on.

Bob Krasnow **on Phil Spector's search for perfection on River Deep, Mountain High** •305

I don't consider Motown black — I consider them half and half. Black people making white music.

Phil Spector •306

Phil had been trying to construct this giant wall of sound ever since he got started in the record business, and when he heard me, he knew that my voice was the final brick.

Ronnie Spector •307

The studio is an instrument, manipulate it, don't go in thinking it's got to sound like my band. When I got done with *Pretty Gate Machine*, I realized, 'Holy fuck, how am I going to play this live?'

Trent Reznor **of Nine Inch Nails, 1996** •308

It's a radical time for musicians, a really revolutionary time, and I believe revolutions like Napster are a lot more fun than cash, which by the way we don't have at major labels anyway, so we might as well get with it and get in the game. *Courtney Love* •309

Treating your audience like thieves is absurd. Anyone who chooses to listen to our music becomes a collaborator.

Jeff Tweedy •310

This is the end of an era in pop music. It's the end of ideology. Everything is branded. It began with the compilation album — music to drive to, music to eat to, — thus denying each artist their own ideological spirit. Pop is now given away with a few Esso coupons at your local garage. *Malcolm McLaren* **The Observer, 1998** •311

Whenever you can buy hamburgers to your favourite songs, you know it's over.

Peter Buck **of R.E.M., circa 1996** •312

If you look at the radio playlists of virtually every commercial station; modern rock, alternative or whatever, there's practically no independent music at all. They don't just say, 'Hey this is cool, we'll play this.' It's a political, calculated thing. It all comes down to label support, and most independent labels don't have the kind of backing it takes to break a record in that environment. *Warren Fitzgerald* **of The Vandals, 2000** •313

Promoting pop music ain't about nothing but whores and blow.

Steve Earle **2000** •314

The key to building a superstar is to keep their mouth shut.
To reveal an artist to the people can be to destroy him.
Bob Ezrin **producer** •315

You've got to be organised to have a career in pop music. The people
who have kept going for a long time, they're all organised — and strong.
Trevor Horn, **The Times, Sept 2009** •316

Every time there was an interview, it was Malcolm
who was being interviewed, not us. And that wasn't
what it was all about. Not for me anyway.
Glen Matlock **in his autobiography, I Was a Teenage Sex Pistol, 1990** •317

If Adam [Ant] was the first of the artists as businessmen then McLaren
was the businessman as artist. He didn't play the guitar, but he did play
the media. More interested in an adventure than a career, he was in some
respects an awful manager. He just didn't care. No good going to him
if you were looking for a future in the pop game. He'd drop you as soon
as he got bored. *Dave Rimmer* •318

Now you can manufacture just about what you want and
after just a little time the artist is forgotten and gone.
Jimmy Cliff •319

It will be massive! It will jump out of the box and go mad. It will explode! Believe me — I know.

Terence Trent D'Arby **predicts great things for his 1989 album Neither Fish Nor Flesh. It sucked and it sunk.** •320

You can never tell if your fans will like an album or if they won't and I'm not gonna sit and try to market myself to anybody.
Billie Joe Armstrong **of Green Day 2001** •321

I've got this brilliant thing where I go, "I'm Robbie Williams", and people are interested in what I want to say — which is amazing because I'm just an idiot from Stoke-on-Trent.
Robbie Williams, **1999** •322

By MTV trying to visualise the music they automatically stripped it of most of its natural mystery and depth. Before rock video, when people were confronted by the music, they had to rely on their own natural ability to utilise their imagination.

Neil Young **1990** •323

I think you're in trouble if your videos
are better than your songs. *Boy George* •324

Rock journalism is people who can't
write interviewing people who can't
talk for people who can't read.

Frank Zappa •325

I see a lot of people willingly and unwillingly having
idiosyncrasies in their lives magnified into freak
elements simply to land the cover of magazines.
Bob Mould of Sugar, ex-Husker Du, 1996 •326

There is nothing at all the matter
with some journalists that a quick
slap in the face couldn't sort out.

Elvis Costello 1995 •327

Most journalists shouldn't have a job. Most papers
are a waste of time. A waste of trees. Futile. I'd
rather read a tree. You'd even get bowel cancer
if you use those papers as toilet roll.

Shane MacGowan 1989 •328

If you give one magazine an interview, then the other
magazine wants an interview. If you give one to one,
then the other one wants one. So pretty soon, you're in
the interview business... You're just giving interviews...

Bob Dylan 1969 •329

The media over-estimates its own
importance. I was on the cover of
everything for three years, but I still only
had half a bottle of milk in the fridge.

Mark E Smith of The Fall •330

Download culture isn't a very romantic experience for the fan regarding
art. It cheapens it, makes it fast-forwardable, disposable and ignorable.

Jack White •331

Fame makes a man take things over,
Fame lets him loose, hard to swallow,
Fame puts you there where things are hollow.

David Bowie Fame, (co-written with John Lennon) (1975)
from the album Young Americans •332

The Doors, in their success, did little more
than pretend to provoke the imagination.
They were wholly and obviously synthetic.

Sandy Pearlman •333

I think when you become successful it's very easy to step over and become product, and that has never happened and will never happen to me. *Morrissey* circa 1994 •334

Celebrity fucks people up. Celebrity knocks the stuffing out of people, personally and creatively. There's not much that fucks you up faster than celebrity and isolation.
George Michael Bare magazine, 1988 •335

Fame hits you really hard, like a fucking juggernaut.
You deal with it two ways. Drink and drugs.
Noel Gallagher, Mojo, Jan 2009 •336

It's kind of hip to complain about success.
Scott Weiland of Stone Temple Pilots 1993 •337

If you're in jazz and more than ten people like you, you're labelled commercial.

Herbie Mann •338

Fame, on its best day, is kind of like a friendly wave from the stranger by the side of the road. And when it's not so good, it's like a long walk home, all alone, with nobody in when you get there.
Bruce Springsteen circa 1985 •339

I don't want to be recognized, I don't want to be hassled.
I just want to play guitar in a rock and roll band.

Chrissie Hynde **of The Pretenders 1995 •340**

I'm famous now because of unhappiness.
Your misery is everyone else's entertainment.

Adam Duritz **of Counting Crows 1994 •341**

It's all a bit overwhelming and I just need
to chill out at home. I wasn't born yesterday,
but I didn't realize how cutthroat it was.

Gavin Rossdale **of Bush 1996 •342**

The very weird religion of celebrity scares me. It's like people are creating fake heroes
because they don't have any real ones. The politicians have failed us, religion has
failed as, so who do people turn to? Celebrities. It is wrong. *Michael Stipe* **1992 •343**

I get worried about the scale of success. Because
basically I'm a very private person and I don't get
a thrill from seeing my picture in the paper.

Mike Scott **of The Waterboys •344**

It's not like if The Jam had failed I could go and lay carpets.
I'd be totally fucked. I'd probably still be sat in the pub on the
estate, getting drunk.
Paul Weller March 2006 •345

I don't feel guilty for
being rich and famous.
Sting 1996 •346

Just because you're successful,
doesn't make you any wiser.
The Edge •347

As soon as you get any success you disappear
up your own arse — and lose it forever.
Thom Yorke •348

I always wished for this, but it's
almost turning into more of
anightmare than a dream.
Eminem on the price of fame •349

I used to be afraid of being in my 40s. Now I find out my 40s are pretty good. Of course, I'm rich and I'm married to Christie Brinkley, and that will tend to skew one's view of things.

Billy Joel •350

If this CD fails it's
Strictly Come Dancing
then straight to panto.

Robbie Williams, 2009 •351

Financially, I want to be big in America, because that means I'll never have to work again. But it's not important to me to be a big star. It's more important to be big in England, because that's where I live, that's where I come from.

Noel Gallager of Oasis, 1996 •352

All artists go through a period of turmoil where they turn on success or success turns on them. Most of them can't ride that out. I guess I was fortunate in that I had been playing and singing for 13 years when success came. It touched me deeply but it didn't make me crazy.

Roy Orbison 1988 •353

We've always known that we'd be huge stars, and it's all we wanted, so it won't surprise us when it happens. We don't want to be known as some fucking spaced out Mancunians who've got nothing better to do than take drugs and make music.
Ian Brown **of The Stone Roses, 1989** •354

His big stumbling block has been the problem that every major pop success faces and hardly anyone solves: when you've made your millions, when you've cut your monsters, when your peak has just been passed, what happens next? What about the 50 years before you die?
Nik Cohn **on Phil Spector** •355

There's no point in success if you don't let it go to your head. That's what it's for.
John Otway **1990** •356

It's a great story, isn't it? Loads of potential and, er, screwed up dramatically.

John Perry of The Only Ones •357

120

A lot of people don't like the road, but it's as natural to me as breathing.
I do it because I'm driven to do it, and I either hate it or love it. I'm mortified
to be on the stage, but then again, it's the only place where I'm happy.
Bob Dylan 1997 •358

> I love my job. I love the position I'm in. I love all
> the benefits that come with it, but I still hate touring.
> *Michael Stipe* of R.E.M. 1994 •359

Onstage, I've been hit by a grapefruit, beer cans, eggs, spit, money, cigarette butts,
mandies, Quaaludes, joints, bras, panties and a fist. *Iggy Pop* 1986 •360

> I love to hear the crowd sing along. I get the biggest hard-on from that.
> Of course, it means I have an erection for a whole hour every night.
> *Chester Bennington* of Linkin Park 2001 •361

When I'm on the stage, I'm not in control of myself at all. I don't even
know who I am. I'm not this rational person who can sit here now and
talk to you. If you walked on the stage with a microphone in the middle
of the concert, I'd probably come close to killing you.
> *Pete Townshend* 1982 •362

> It was good fun except old Van is such a miserable old fucker.
> It's amazing 'cos he got us on that tour. We were right down there
> on the list, but it was him who got us on. But d'you know, not once
> on that tour did he ever just poke his head round the dressing-room
> door and say, 'All right fellas?'
>
> *Nick Lowe* 1979 •363

We can't stop touring because we
like it so much. I believe I'm going
nuts at times — but so what?
Ozzy Osbourne in his Black Sabbath days •364

The funny thing about touring is that you rehearse all the
wrong things: the music, the stage show. That stuff isn't the
problem, it's the other 22 hours of the day. That's the weird part.

Michael Hutchence in 1991 •365

It's nice that you can go to any country, and all these people have been waiting
to see you for six months, they bought the ticket ages ago. It's quite moving really.
But it's strange when you come back to your little life in London.

Darryl Hunt of The Pogues in 1991 •366

One of the papers said what a sad existence I must have, that
I don't have a social life. But I do have a social life. Our floor in
the hotel is like a little street in suburbia. We all pop in to see
each other and have a cup of tea. It's just like when I was living
in a squat, only now I make a lot more money.

Boy George on tour in Japan •367

The ultimate sin of any performer is contempt for the audience.

Lester Bangs in Village Voice, 1977 •368

If you ever plan to motor west
Travel my way, take the highway that's the best
And get your kicks on Route 66.
Route 66, written by *Bobby Troup* performed by many •369

Would you put your lighters away?
You're not at Elton John.
Noel Gallagher at Earl's Court in 1995,
as Oasis play the anthemic Wonderwall •370

Americans want grungy fucking people, stabbing
themselves in the head on stage. They get a bright
bunch like us, with deodorant on, they don't get it.
Liam Gallagher in 1997 •371

It means going into training. Then on
the wagon for three months. I knew
when I got back on stage, I'd enjoy it.
But performing's like sex. You might like
it, but you don't want to do it non-stop.
Mick Jagger in 1981 •372

If it wasn't the feeling I get while performing,
I think it would have been impossible for me
to have continued as long as I have.
Chuck Berry in his autobiography •373

124

There's nothing like being on stage. You can't put it in words. When the lights hit you, there's a certain spirit you feel. I don't like coming off!
Michael Jackson •374

That's one of the best feelings on the market, when you walk up the steps to the stage. It feels like sparks flying through you. I get tears in my eyes and — I know this sounds really schmaltzy — but I just want to give.
Michael Hutchence •375

It's a pretty cool feeling going out there and seeing 70,000 smiling faces. Greatest feeling in the world.
Jon Bon Jovi •376

With it's dozen strong dance troupe, set piece dialogues, elaborate costumes and multiple sets, including a Metropolis-style futuristic nightmare, a cathedral, a harem and a Thirties nightclub, Madonna's *Blonde Ambition* is a Broadway musical in all essentials except for its lack of plot. **Charles Shaar Murray** in 1990 •377

I tried to make the show accommodate my own short attention span.
Madonna on the same show •378

When we first started playing, I'd go into every show expecting
nobody to come, and I'd go on stage expecting nobody to give
me anything for free. And that's the way you have to play. If you
don't play like that, pack your guitar up, throw it in a trash can and
go home, fix televisions or some other line of work, ya know?

Bruce Springsteen in 1981 •379

There are perfectly sane men and women who will
tell you that those first Rainbow Roxy Music concerts
changed their lives; the presentation, the cleverness,
the stylisation, the audience. *Peter York* •380

Olympia is like many large concert venues: when fully packed it closely
resembles the concentration camp scenes in Wertmuller's *Seven Beauties*.
A greyish darkness piled with sullen, lumpy half dead whelps.

Lester Bangs at a Wings concert in 1976 •381

The Waterboys crowd is a riotous assembly of time
warped punks, stubbly young men of poetic aspect in
loose-fitting shirts and long hair, people clearly familiar
with the clubs and pubs where traditional music is played,
and others who can only be described as parents. All that
was really lacking was a Guinness fountain.

Adam Sweeting in 1989 •382

126

Being on tour sends me crazy, I drink too much
and out comes the John McEnroe in me.
The Pretenders' *Chrissie Hynde* •383

Pop concerts are just gatherings of people who want
to have a good time and I don't think they really have
a higher meaning. *Mick Jagger* 1968 •384

I don't want to be a caricature of myself.

Singer *Tom Jones* **asks women not to throw underwear at him during concerts** •385

Things do sometimes get a little out of hand around me. I remember
this show where I was grabbed and held down, while one chick was
trying to pull my pants down. Some others were trying to french kiss me.
And another one used her mouth on me. All the time I'd be kicking one,
hitting another. I like to fight chicks. It turns me on.

Iggy Pop 1972 •386

I really do love performing. I mean it, it's totally
natural to me, I'm a dandy, a show-off. I get
very high on all the attention. I love it.
Freddie Mercury 1974 •387

If I leave the stage feeling, 'Well if I played just one more song, maybe somebody out there would be won over', if I feel I could have given more it's hard for me to sleep that night.

Bruce Springsteen 1981 •388

I couldn't talk to people face to face, so I got on stage and started screaming and squealing and twitching.

David Byrne •389

When the Heads started speaking French, The Ramones plunged to the depths of misery and horror.

Tom Verlaine **on an uneasy touring bus shared by The Ramones and Talking Heads** •390

I think you have a duty to perform, you have to entertain people. But just 'cos someone might wear a sequinned jacket onstage does not mean that they are instantly interesting to watch.

Jarvis Cocker •391

With Dire Straits, it was so damn big. You're a part of a travelling circus.
The lighting rig came from *Star Trek*. When we got to the point of carrying
around our own stage, I decided I had had enough.

Mark Knopfler 2000 •392

On stage, I make love to 25,000 different people, then I go home alone.

Janis Joplin •393

It's not the first time I have died in Coventry.

Former Fairport Convention violinist *Dave Swarbrick*
after reading his obituary in The Daily Telegraph •394

Usually, when we come off stage, there
are people waiting with towels, drinks…
Here, I fell over and no one gave a toss.

Spandau Ballet's *Gary Kemp* **on Live Aid** •395

We did this show with Nirvana at the Warfield in San Francisco. They plugged in and from the first chord, Kurt flew into the audience. He was surfing the crowd while playing the song. The crowd threw him back onto the stage, and he hit the first line of the vocal. I was like, 'Fuck it, there is no way we can beat that'.

Thurston Moore of Sonic Youth, 1994 •396

Most of the time you really don't know where you are. It's very possible that you may come out on stage and say, 'It's great to be here in St. Louis' and you could very well be in Denver or Seattle. That's happened. *Tom Waits* 1985 •397

(a) Cauliflower and broccoli, cut into individual florets and thrown immediately into the garbage. I fucking hate that.

(b) One case of big bottles of good, premium beer. You decide. But remember, I might ask you to taste a bottle, so buy something nice. Here's a clue — it probably won't start with the letter "B" and end with "udweiser".

(c) 120-volt electrical service in each (dressing room). Which normally means a really iffy-looking wall socket that's already got three things plugged into it, one of which is the entire stage lighting rig. But let's hope this time it's different…

From roadie Jos Grain's rider to an Iggy Pop tour; it is a work of comic genius •398

My advice to people today is as follows: if you take the
game of life seriously, if you take your nervous system seriously,
if you take your sense organs seriously, if you take the energy
process seriously, you must turn on, tune in, and drop out.
Timothy Leary 1966, published in **The Politics of Ecstasy** •399

As far as I can see, the history of experimental art
in the twentieth century is intimately bound up
with the experience of intoxification.
Will Self The Face, 1994 •400

If you remember the 1960s,
you weren't there. *George Harrison* •401

I had taken some strong psychedelics right before
I went on stage. I was struggling to keep myself
grounded. My guitar was like rubber.
Carlos Santana of the Woodstock experience •402

I don't know if I've been lucky or it's that
subconscious careful, but I've never turned
blue in someone's bathroom. I consider
that the height of bad manners.
Keith Richard shows admirable breeding •403

I got registered as an addict, which is really the first step to getting out. Because the first thing you have to do is admit you're on the stuff, which you tend not to do. I spent at least three years pretending I wasn't a junkie, that I didn't really 'need' heroin. Which is nonsense. And when you have to go to a clinic every day to pick it up, along with all the other junkies, then you know. *Marianne Faithfull* 1978 •404

Nobody stopped thinking about those psychedelic experiences. Once you've been to some of those places, you think, 'How can I get back there again but make it a little easier on myself.' *Jerry Garcia* of The Grateful Dead, Rolling Stone, 01989 •405

Going into rehab became a habit, something to break the boredom, like cigarettes. When things got bad at home I'd get raging drunk, pass out and then spend ten days in rehab. *Ronnie Spector* •406

It's not what isn't, it's what you wish was that makes unhappiness… I think I think too much, that's why I drink. *Janis Joplin* •407

I never get drunk. Two drinks and
I get a headache and fall asleep. *Lou Reed* •408

I think the biggest misconception about me is that
I'm a moron, a drunk who can't put my trousers on.
Shane MacGowan ex-Pogues 1995 •409

It's ridiculous. Some people still see us as a drunken
novelty act even after four albums and seven years
and Christ knows how many successful tours.
Spider Stacy **of The Pogues** •410

Sometimes I feel really guilty complaining about it because
there are some amazing things happening around me but
the darkness has prevailed, to be honest, in extremis.
Pete Doherty **shows a rare glimmer of regret in 2006** •411

People talk about this great talent but
there's nothing to him. He's a mess.
Damon Albarn **has no sympathy for the wastrel Doherty** •412

I was happy in the haze of a drunken hour,
But heaven knows I'm miserable now.
The Smiths **Heaven Knows I'm Miserable Now**
(Morrissey/Johnny Marr) (1984) from the album The Smiths •413

I don't need help because if I can't help myself I can't be helped.
Prophetic words from *Amy Winehouse* •414

What's the point of going to college if you can't drink beer?

John Homme **of Queens Of The Stone Age, 2000** •415

I loved being in Hawkwind… it was like Star Trek with long hair and drugs.

Lemmy, **2007** •416

That was the old days when you could get the good stuff…
I'll always prefer speed to cocaine: cocaine makes you
think you're gonna throw up, wears off too quick and
you go to sleep on it. What's the point of that?
Said *Lemmy,* **with a nostalgic sigh.** •417

The Replacements gave me a new respect for drinking.
They took drinking a lot to this new art form level
— not about being a total idiot, but about being
this beautiful perfect drunk.
Billie Joe Armstrong **of Green Day 1996** •418

If I had my way I would have sex, drugs and rock and roll at least four to six hours a day.
Perry Farrell **of Jane's Addition,** circa 1993 •419

I spent most of the Eighties, most of my life, riding around in somebody else's car, in possession of, or ingested of, something illegal, on my way from something illegal to something illegal with many illegal things happening all around me. *Iggy Pop* **The Guardian, 1996** •420

I can honestly say, all the bad things that ever happened to me were directly attributed to drugs and alcohol. I mean, I would never urinate at the Alamo at nine o'clock in the morning dressed in a woman's evening dress sober. *Ozzy Osbourne* **1992** •421

Everything I've ever loved was immoral, illegal or grew hair on your palms.
Steven Tyler **of Aerosmith** •422

It details how she started out as a prostitute, got addicted to heroin, and eventually became a successful singer. And if you read it backwards, it doubles as a biography of Courtney Love.
Mark Lamarr **on a biography of Billie Holliday** •423

Kids, don't buy drugs. Wait until you're a rock star and they give them to you free.

Bill Nighy as *Billy Mack* **Love Actually (writer: Richard Curtis), 2003** •424

Ecstasy is a drug so strong it makes white people think they can dance.

Lenny Henry •425

Think of what you could do with all the money they spend trying to fight drugs. Legalize them. Take the profit and the glamour out of them.

Lou Reed 1989 •426

Mushrooms make me too fucking giggly. I just laugh at everything. I don't like to laugh too much.

Eminem 2000 •427

My first drug experience was sniffing glue. We tried it, and moved on to Carbona. That's why we wrote songs about it. It was a good high, but it gave you a bad high. I guess it destroys your brain cells. *Johnny Ramone* 2001 •428

I'll never stop smoking pot. I'm a drug addict and always fucking will be. I like my pot.

Shaun Ryder of The Happy Mondays 1991 •429

When I found drugs, I thought I'd found the greatest thing. All you do is snort this shit up your nose or stick this needle in your arm, and you're a fucking genius.

Flea of The Red Hot Chili Peppers 1995 •430

I heard that your brain stops growing when you start doing drugs. Let's see, I guess that makes me 19.

Steven Tyler of Aerosmith, 1979 •431

I've never had problems with drugs. I've had problems with the police.

Mick Jagger of Rolling Stones 1999 •432

I've got no time for drugs any more… I tried them all and wouldn't recommend any of them.

Mick Jagger •433

I felt in retrospect that getting rid of the drugs allowed the real problems to surface. It allowed light to come into a lot of dark corners, and then you had to deal with the real issues that the drugs had just been covering up. That's a process of several years.

Roseanne Cash •434

All I can say is that drugs are a retreat. Artistic people are by nature so volatile, and if you're highly strung, which I am, you're vulnerable. *Boy George* 1989 •435

They shoulda called me Little Cocaine,
I was sniffing so much of the stuff. My
nose got big enough to back a diesel truck
in, unload it, and drive it right out again.

Little Richard reminisces •436

In the case of heroin, the drug's failure for Eric was not to live
up to his expectations in helping to create some work of
genius, or help him towards some profound recognition of life.
Ray Coleman on Eric Clapton, 1985 •437

It makes me feel like a fly with its wings stuck in honey.

Captain Beefheart on dope •438

If I'd had a happy childhood and my dad hadn't
been an alcoholic drug addict, there'd have been
no angst and no songs. I'd be an accountant or
something and I'd be dying of boredom.

Nikki Six of Motley Crue •439

How I got to be a psychedelic guru was I just appointed myself one. Basically, all you have to do to become one is take enough drugs.

Lux Interior of The Cramps, 1980 •440

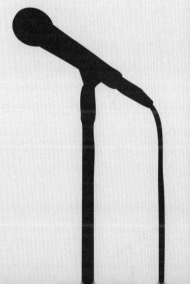

Style's not something that you decide on
Monday and photograph on Thursday. You've
been developing that for your whole life.
Simon Le Bon •441

For a start, the band is much more
handsome since I joined.
Sid Vicious •442

What was so good about the 60s was that we had so many
great dressers to copy. Every time I saw Brian Jones with
some new trousers I had to get some. *Patti Smith* •443

Punk was just a way to sell trousers.
Malcolm McLaren •444

I remember standing in front of the stage waiting
for them to come on, and McLaren coming down the
stairs with Vivienne Westwood, and she was wearing
the first bondage suit I'd ever seen. And I thought,
'fucking hell! What is that?' It was quite striking.
Pat Collier of The Vibrators on a 100 Club gig •445

I got a pair of salmon pink jeans and ran 'em up on my
mum's sewing machine. They used to stop traffic.
Pete Shelley of The Buzzcocks •446

144

When we started we wanted some kind of definite anti-glitter look, 'cos that what was going on then. It's amazing how they've changed punk rock bands into glitter. I mean these clothing stores that sold glitter stuff are now selling the same stuff, but now it's punk fashions. *Johnny Ramone* •447

Of course we are big fans of Roxy Music. Inside the first album, Roxy Music, you learn what a really cool 70s rock and roll outfit means. Platform boots, tight jacket. Wahoo!
Jean-Benoit Dunckel of Air 2001 •448

I mean, in a couple of years time, I'll probably look at a picture of me in platforms and say, 'What the hell was I doing?'
Elton John 1973 •449

In England, glamour's in the gutter, it's everywhere, anywhere you want to find it.
Boy George Smash Hits, 1982 •450

Boy George is all England needs — another queen who can't dress.
Joan Rivers •451

I'd like the band to be remembered as a good band, not as a funny old drag queen in a hat with some silly pop songs.
Boy George on Culture Club •452

I like a suit but I don't look right in a suit. I put a suit on, my face just don't go with the suit, man. My face — I just ain't got a suit face. It's too bumpy. Weird.

Bruce Springsteen 1975 •453

Bryan Ferry is the only popular music star to have mastered the visual grammar of Jermyn Street, the only one ever to have worn a real tweed jacket.

Peter York •454

My relationship with rock and roll is like Lenny Bruce's with modern jazz — I like the clothes and the attitude.

John Cooper Clarke •455

I love wearing them to Elton John's annual bash because mine are nicer than his. I'm a Chevalier, a knight, a sheikh and a Prince Tuareg in Western Sudan. I look like Idi Amin when I've got them all on.

Bob Geldof **makes light of his medal collection, 2001** •456

I have to be honest — the first time I saw Cher, I thought she was a hooker. *Ronnie Spector* •457

A certain amount of uplift and control, just what a bouncing boy needs when dressed in tights on stage.

Ian Anderson **justifies his codpiece** •458

I'm a size queen right? Honestly, I am, I can't lie. My friends sometimes say, 'you know, Janet, its not always about the size, but the magic in the wand.' And I'm like, 'but there's nothing wrong with a big magic wand.'
Janet Jackson 2001 •459

Let's face it, if I was a dentist it wouldn't be quite the same. If there are uglier guys around I don't know where they are, and yet I am the King of Pussy!
Gene Simmons •460

Chicks all dig the Wolf. They all dig the Wolf. Because he is a mighty wolf, he's a mountain wolf, he wipes out his tracks.
Howlin' Wolf obviously disputes Gene's claim •461

It was huge. At that time, it was the reason I did everything. It's the reason I played the guitar — because of my nose. The reason I write songs was because of my nose.
Pete Townshend 1968 •462

David Byrne would qualify as an artist.
I mean, by appearance's sake. He looks
like he's dying.

David Lee Roth •463

I know I look ridiculous sometimes, absolutely idiotic,
but remember, when I started out I was quite rotund.

Elton John 1976 •464

Elvis Costello is terrible, all fat
and sweaty. Can't dance either.

Ian McCulloch •465

I don't want to be one of those middle-aged guys who
turns up with the baseball hat on the wrong way round.
Elvis Costello •466

What he's doing is what I desperately wanted to do,
which is to age with dignity in this business.
Pete Townshend on Eric Clapton, 1985 •467

I'd hate to go down in history as the man who
spawned a thousand Goth bands. *Nick Cave* •468

I always had denied I was a Goth. Then again, looking back on titles like
Sacrilege and *Serpent's Kiss*, I guess the weight of evidence is against me.
Wayne Hussey **of The Mission** •469

All you Goths can fuck off back to your tents.
The Mission aren't on 'till tomorrow.
Bernard Sumner **of New Order 2001** •470

We use white light — coloured lights are for Christmas trees.
Peter Murphy **of Bauhaus** •471

It's my life and my body, and if I want to fuck myself up
and have a beard and wear my hair long, that's my business.
Elvis Costello **1991** •472

Long hair is an unpardonable offence which should be punishable by death.

Morrissey •473

I could've hosted *The Generation Game*. Or *3-2-1*. I could've done anything in 1984.

Morrissey **on stardom** •474

I had black hair so people said we were goth.
Now I have red hair so people say we're glam.
Marilyn Manson **1998** •475

Blonde is just a state of mind. You definitely have more fun. I've been so popular since I dyed my hair.

Lou Reed 1974 •476

Once I went blonde, there was no turning back. And when the roots began to show, I just got too lazy to deal with it, and people loved it even more.

Debbie Harry 1977 •477

Paul Weller just stole everything. He's a skinny twat who has the worst haircut going.

Ian McCulloch •478

I was a skinhead years ago. This was before punk and just after mods. I was 15. Then I became a 'Suedehead' because I grew my hair some. After that I was a 'casual,' which meant your hair was longer still. Everything was defined by your hair.

Bernard Sumner of New Order 1993 •479

If Britney Spears would paint her ass green,
I'm sure you could spot green asses all over
LA. As soon as the word was out.
Billie Joe Armstrong of Green Day 2000 •480

Everyone wants to look like
her. A chick with a dick.
Cheryl Cole on the tom-boy charms
of Lily Allen •481

Taking your clothes off, doing sexy dancing
and marrying a rich footballer must be so gratifying.
Your mother must be so proud. *Lily Allen* responds •482

I don't see why there has to be an age limit
to performing rap. There's no age limit in
rock — for fuck's sake look at Kiss! *Ice-T* •483

In art or theatre or literature, nobody says
"I'm sorry, pal, you're 45, you've got to spend
the rest of your life reading the same book or
seeing the same film or going to the same play."
John Peel on listening to new music •484

I love romance! I love being treated like
a princess. I think all women should be.

Kylie 2001 •485

> Well it ain't no secret
> I've been around a time or two.
> Well I don't know baby maybe
>   you've been around too.
> Well there's another dance
> All you gotta do is say yes
> And if you're rough and ready for love
> Honey I'm tougher than the rest.

Bruce Springsteen Tougher Than The Rest (1987)
from the album Tunnel Of Love •486

Adolescents tend to be passionate people, and
passion is no less real because it is directed
towards a hot-rod, a commercialised popular
singer, or the leader of a black-jacketed gang.

Canadian educationist and sociologist *Edgar Z Friedenberg* 1959 •487

The Stone Roses album, I really like it, but it's all singing about she this and she that... never write songs about girls.

Ian McCulloch •488

Guys would sleep with a bicycle if it had the right colour lip gloss on. They have no shame. They're like bull elks in a field. *Tori Amos* •489

I didn't lose my virginity until I was 18. The first time was a nightmare. Who shows you how to use a condom?

Adam Ant •490

If I was a girl, I'd rather fuck
a rock star than a plumber.

Gene Simmons of Kiss, circa 1986 •491

You get used to being a sex god.

Dave Gedge of The Wedding Present 1992 •492

I got a pair of red, synthetic satin women's pants
through the post the other day with a phone number
on. That was quite strange. I haven't tried the phone
number. In times of stress I may. *Jarvis Cocker* •493

I'm the only genuine sex symbol
in the current pop scene.

So said *Ian McCulloch* in the 1980s •494

155

I thought everybody in rock
had illegitimate children.

Rod Stewart •495

I think Mick Jagger would
be astounded and amazed if
he realised to how many people
he is not a sex symbol.

Angie Bowie •496

As far as I'm concerned, the benefit
of being a black Irishman is that I
pull more chicks. *Phil Lynott* Thin Lizzy •497

I'm very healthy and natural when it comes to sex. Strange locations always turn me on. Aeroplane toilets. I think that would turn anybody on. *Bjork* 1996 •498

In our minds, love and lust are really separated. It's hard to find someone that can be kind and you can trust enough to leave your kids with, and isn't afraid to throw her man up against the wall and lick him from head to toe. *Tori Amos* •499

For me, rock and roll is all about when you're in a bar and you're in love with someone and you want to fuck them and a band's playing. *Mark Eitzel* of American Music Club 1994 •500

Anything can be sex. Getting off is sex. Getting to an audience is sex. Looking is sex. Your body is a framework with infinite possibilities.

Lou Reed 1975 •501

It all stems from Nico actually. She was the one who took me when I was a skinny little naive brat and taught me how to eat pussy and all about the best French wines and German champagnes.

Iggy Pop •502

I prefer snogging and petting to full sex
— it leaves more to the imagination.

Jarvis Cocker of Pulp 1995 •503

I've never taken advantage of one night stands. It's like treating sex like sneezing. Sex is a fairly disgusting sort of tufted, smelly-area kind of activity, which is too intimate to engage in with strangers.

Thom Yorke of Radiohead 1995 •504

Sex? I'd rather have a cup of tea.
Boy George •505

Sometimes a woman can really persuade you to make an asshole of yourself.

Rod Stewart 2001 •506

I've actually broken up with boyfriends for inspiration. When I hit a period of not being able to write music, I walk away.
Lily Allen, 2009 •507

I threw out the love songs. I want visceral energy, not piano ballads.

Nick Cave •508

The other night, this guy gave me head. I'm not gay. I don't think so, anyway. I don't know. I just wanted to see what it felt like. And you know, he stunk. I thought 'it's going to be good, because he's a guy.' He went at it like he was eating corn on the cob or something.

Perry Farrell of Jane's Addiction 1991 •509

I see myself as a bisexual man who's never had a homosexual experience.

Brett Anderson of Suede 1993 •510

If I decide to have sex with a man, I'm not sure that I absolutely have to be a gay role model.

Bob Mould of Sugar, ex-Husker Du 1994 •511

Them lot, I think they fancy me. I think they're all gay.

Liam Gallagher's eloquent appraisal of the press •512

There are four hundred million sperm in each ejaculation — and if you look around, take a look at some people, it's kinda hard to imagine that they beat four hundred million. It makes one wonder.

Tom Waits 1999 •513

Maybe the most you can expect from a relationship that goes bad is to come out of it with a few good songs.

Marianne Faithfull on the disintegration of her relationship with Mick Jagger •514

He's a great father and a great friend. Just a lousy husband.

Jerry Hall on former husband Mick Jagger •515

I was so struck by the fact
that your heart does break.

Bob Geldof on breaking up with Paula Yates •516

Curtis has an astonishing gift for
words, steering well clear of the usual
"ma bay-bee done left me" of the rock
relationship-breakdown song, singing
words that smell of decay and tense
silence, betrayal and buried violence.

Gary Mulholland on Joy Division's Love Will Tear Us Apart (from This
Is Uncool, the 500 Greatest Singles Since Punk and Disco) •517

I just see monogamy in a different way
to most people. I don't think it's a terrible
thing to have sex with someone else. I think
it's much worse to substitute the man in your
life with another person. It's hard to explain
but things like taking another man to your
mum's house or going out shopping with
him are so rude, and worse than kissing
him. Sex is just sex, but you should never
let anyone else get close.

Amy Winehouse •518

Feminists should be concerned about the personalities in rock and roll because they will be the primary means by which young women get the feminist message.

Camille Paglia controversial cultural critic, 1995 •519

Women are going to be the new Elvises. That's the only place for rock 'n' roll to go.

Debbie Harry in prime Blondie days •520

> She always had a great sense of humour about all
> the attention… she was (and is) a face for the ages.
> And a pretty good singer and songwriter as a bonus.
> *Mick Rock* **on Debbie Harry, 1984 •521**

Debbie's persona, innocent yet sluttish, arrogant yet
waif-like, was consciously rooted in America's most
mystical of all sex objects.   *Philip Norman* **on Debbie Harry's**
deference to Marilyn •522

> Sadly, Blondie will never be a star simply because she ain't
> good enough, but for the time being I hope she's having fun.
> *Charles Shaar Murray* **makes a crap prediction in 1975 •523**

I just felt that being forty two years old and not
being size zero, and not being blonde, that it could
be a really positive statement for a woman.

Belinda Carlisle **on appearing naked in Playboy in 2001 •524**

It was a real cheap publicity stunt.

Nancy Sinatra **is a little more sanguine about her own appearance**
in the same magazine in 1995 •525

I'm chuffed. I have two fantastic kids and I don't have to work. I figure I've made a fuck of a lot of noise in my life, so now is my time to be quiet. My worst nightmare would be for me to go out there and for every cab driver to think they knew who I was. I don't know you and you don't know me. Great. Let's keep it simple and tidy.

Chrissie Hynde in Mojo, 2006 •526

Back before the flood, when Patti Smith began caterwauling poetry above an electric guitar, she probably didn't realise she was clearing the path for legions of bad-tempered demoiselles with dark clothing and three-subject notebooks full of lousy poems.

Steve Anderson in Village Voice, 1982 •527

Patti Smith has an aura that'd probably show up under ultraviolet light. She can generate more intensity with a single movement of one hand than most rock performers can produce in an entire set.

Charles Shaar Murray •528

We attract groupies of both sexes. The girls
are far more forward in their suggestiveness.
Donita Sparks of L7 •529

My philosophy on life is that I'm not about my
external appearance. What I have to say it's far
more important than how long my eyelashes are.
Alanis Morissette •530

We feel like the girls in *Sex and
the City*. Without the sex.
Cheryl Cole of Girls Aloud on living the life. •531

I created Punk for this day and age. Do you see Britney
walking around wearing ties and singing punk? Hell no.
That's what I do. I'm like a Sid Vicious for a new generation.
Avril Lavigne •532

When I was growing up
I thought Kim Deal was the
most brilliant woman in rock.

Shirley Manson on the Pixies'
bassist, 1996 •533

When I started, I got a lot
of attention because I was
aggressive, strident. People
liked that. *Shirley Manson*
of Garbage 1999 •534

I don't mean to be a diva, but some days
you wake up and you're Barbra Streisand.
Courtney Love •535

Whatever I wore, whatever I did,
people were putting this incredible
emphasis of sexuality on me.
Kate Bush, the most un-pop-star of pop stars •536

I don't want to do anything that's just straight glamorous.
It has to have some element of uneasiness or humour.
P.J. Harvey •537

I think people are always going to think the worst of me.
They're ready and willing to cast me into these dark holes,
to say that I'm this physically and mentally unstable character.
So I have to be careful not to present them with such
an easy target. *P.J. Harvey* 1997 •538

She sang like a rock 'n' roll banshee and leapt about
the stage like a dervish. It *was* the raunchiest, grittiest,
most attacking rhythm and blues singing I'd ever heard.
Michael Thomas on Janis Joplin in Ramparts, 1967 •539

Janice could scream and squall just as hard as Tina,
but Tina could dance. Janice couldn't. I couldn't.
We weren't dancers. Tina is like a female James Brown.
She is a mover and she looks good. *Little Richard* •540

Finally, she says, 'okay, Phil, one more time.' And she ripped
her blouse off and grabbed the microphone, and she gave
a performance that… I mean, your hair was standing on
end. It was like the whole room exploded. I'll never forget
that as long as I live, man. It was a magic moment.
Bob Krasnow on Tina Turner recording River Deep,
Mountain High, with Phil Spector •541

When she came in, she was electric. We turned
the lights down, just had a couple of sidelights
on each wall. And she couldn't swing with the
song with all her clothes on, so she took her blouse
off and sang it just wearing a bra. What a body!
It was unbelievable, the way she moved around.
Larry Levine recording engineer at the same session •542

He'd lock the door, and then you knew you were gonna get it.
One night in the studio he threw boiling hot coffee in my face.
Said I wasn't singing the way he wanted, that I wasn't trying.
Tina Turner on her abusive relationship with her husband Ike •543

She has a voice that was finally wasted in The Supremes,
a voice with a kind of sleepy snarl in it, or else the pitch
and faint breathlessness of a nervous girl singing for dimes.
Dancing, she is like a wildly animated clothes-horse hung
with quickly-changing gowns and silly hats. *Philip Norman*
on Diana Ross •544

Aretha carries you back to church in everything that she does.
Al Jackson on Aretha Franklin •545

I'm not a raving loony.
I'm a fiery, passionate
woman who cares about
what is happening
in the world.
Sinead O'Connor •546

I could be more in control
but I don't want to be. I'm
always thirsty for surprise.
Bjork •547

I admire that, … but I can't see myself
doing it because I'm a loudmouthed cow.
Charlotte Church after hearing that Celine Dion didn't
speak for a whole day before a concert •548

I just do the same stuff I always did. I have
a bigger apartment — that's the main change.
Norah Jones •549

Dolly Parton's just kind of a
southern magnolia blossom
that floats on the breeze.
Linda Ronstadt •550

I'm not offended at all because
I know I'm not a dumb blonde.
I also know I'm not blonde.
Dolly Parton whips the rug from under
her detractors' feet, 1993 •551

Most people say it would make a wonderful soap opera.
I'm sure it could, but to me it's just my life. *Tammy Wynette* •552

I still think of myself
as an awkward tomboy.
It's something I'll never
get over, no matter how
many magazines I'm in.
Jewel 1998 •553

I learned the truth at seventeen,
That love was meant for beauty queens,
And high school girls with clear skinned smiles,
Who married young and then retired.
Janis Ian At Seventeen (1975) from
the album Between The Lines •554

A typical guy wants the woman under his thumb, like
his housewife and all that, and we're not having it!
Ari Up lead singer of The Slits •555

Don't let anyone tell you that you have to be
a certain way. Be unique. Be what you feel.
Melissa Etheridge •556

You don't have to be age 20 and size zero to
be sexually viable or viable as a woman.
Belinda Carlisle •557

I tell women, 'Go and masturbate! Get loads of kinky books
and masturbate every day!' *They do* it from the age of nine.
Björk NME, 1993 •558

I sometimes worry about
using my lesbianism as a
marketing tool. Let's get over it;
it's my art now. *k.d.lang* •559

For a while, the genre
seemed to be just about
sex and crime. Rappers are
storytellers; the stories don't
need to be true!
Lauryn Hill •560

I'm not a big fan of Tracy Chapman but it's about time that a black woman is allowed
to come across without having to wear a leather skirt where you can see her pubic hair
sticking out. *Terence Trent D'Arby* 1989 •561

'Girl' is not menstruating, 'Girl' is non-orgasmic, 'Girl' is naive,
cute, bratty, unthreatening in her clumsiness and incompetence.
'Girl' is most of all, young. It is vanity in extremes. I have always
called myself a girl, but I am going to stop now.
Courtney Love of Hole, 1994 •562

172

The trouble with some women is that they get
all excited about nothing — and then marry him.
Cher •563

I was perceiving myself as good as a man or
equal to a man and as powerful and I wanted
to look ambiguous because I thought that was
a very interesting statement to make through
the media. *Annie Lennox* •564

You see, if I was a guy, and I was sitting here with a
cigarette in my hand, grabbing my crotch and talking
about how I make music because I like fast cars and fucking
girls, you'd call me a rock star. But when I do it in my music
and in my videos, because I'm a female, because I make pop
music, you're judgmental and you say that it is distracting…
I'm just a rock star. *Lady GaGa* in a 2009 interview, perceives double
standards in the rock press •565

Show me somebody that puts out an album every year
and I'll show you a man who hasn't got two children
and lives at home with them and has to get them up for
school every morning. Oh God, what everyone needs in
this business is a wife. It must be great. I wish I had a
wife. *Chrissie Hynde* 1991 •566

I think I've always behaved as if I were a star. Since I was a kid I have behaved as if somebody owed me something.
Madonna 1990 •567

I went to New York. I had a dream. I wanted to be a big star. I didn't know anybody. I wanted to dance. I wanted to sing. I wanted to do all those things. I wanted to make people happy. I wanted to be famous. I wanted everybody to love me. I wanted to be a star. I worked really hard and my dream came true.
Madonna **on her early aspirations** •568

I'm sexy. How can I avoid it? I'd have to put a bag over my head. But then my voice would come across. And it's sexy.
Madonna •569

I sometimes think I was born to live up to my name. How could I be anything else but what I am, having been named Madonna? I would either have ended up a nun or this. *Madonna* 1992 •570

I know I'm not the greatest singer or dancer, but that doesn't interest me, I'm interested in being provocative and pushing people's buttons.
Madonna •571

Maybe I'm just a gay man inside a woman's body!
Madonna talking on Parkinson, 2005 •572

I think Madonna is particularly revolting. I find it hard to imagine why anyone would want to so cheapen themselves. The things she says are disgusting, and I'd kill anyone who used her kind of language around me.
Whitney Houston 1988 •573

Madonna is closer to organised prostitution than anything else. I mean, the music industry is obviously prostitution anyway, but there are degrees.
Morrissey 1986 •574

I like my pussy. Sometimes I stare at it in the mirror when I'm undressing and wonder what it would look like without any hair like when I was a baby. Sometimes I sit at the edge of the bed and spred my legs. And stare into the mirror and wonder what others see. Sometimes I stick my finger in my pussy and wiggle it around the dark wetness and feel what a cock or a tongue must feel when I'm sitting on it. I pull my finger out and I always taste and smell it. It's hard to describe, it smells like a baby to me, fresh and full of life.
Madonna **in her Sex book** •575

I'm tough and I'm ambitious and I know exactly what I want. If that makes me a bitch — okay. *Madonna* •576

No one knows how to work this business like she does.
Cher **on Madonna** •577

The thing about Madonna is that she is the ultimate consumer of pop culture. *Malcolm McLaren* •578

She is the self-sufficient postmodern phenomenon. A masterpiece of controlled illusion. *Martin Amis*, 1992, **on Madonna.** •579

Madonna is the speedboat, and the rest of us are just the Go-Go's on water skis. *Liz Phair* **on Madonna** •580

Madonna is more than a celebrity; she is the perfect hybrid that personifies the decadently greedy, selfish sexual decade that spawned her — a corporation in the form of flesh.
Kevin Sessum **1990** •581

You mean they don't realise I'm a songwriter as well as a slut?
Madonna 1989 •582

I don't mind that I see her face on every magazine cover; I don't mind that she is obscene; I don't even mind that she can't sing, can't dance, can't act and is none the less the most famous person on the planet. What I can't stand is that she thinks she is an artist. *Michael Ignatieff*, 1994. •583

An entertainer is a whole different thing, an entertainer to me doesn't necessarily deal with reality. It's someone who makes you forget. It's like a drug, it's euphoric and I think it has its place in the world. But that's not the only thing I do. I think I'm an educator — and I do think I'm an artist.
Madonna •584

The result is *The Madonna Collection*, a collection of academic essays about Madonna that is alternately intriguing and infuriating. It's like watching a group of lecherous monks discuss a porn film in Latin.
Robert Worth in The Guardian, 1992 •585

I won't be happy until I'm as famous as God.

Madonna •586

All I ever wanted was to work for
Radio 1 — it was the realisation
of my life's ambition. And now
I'm here it's completely crap.

Chris Evans, 1992 •587

A lot of pop music is about stealing
pocket money from children.

Ian Anderson of Jethro Tull, Rolling Stone, 1989 •588

I'll grow old physically, but I won't grow old musically

Cliff Richard the Peter Pan of Pop •589

I'm just a normal, everyday kind of Goddess.

Sandie Shaw 1988 •590

In many ways I never felt like
I fitted into all that L.A. lifestyle.
I was too much of a fucking yob.

Rod Stewart •591

I love the fact that Rod's turned into
such a twit — I can surprise people
when I play his early 70's records.

Robert Elms on Rod Stewart's decline, The Word, 2006 •592

The worst part of being gay
in the twentieth century is all
that damn disco music to
which one has to listen.
Quentin Crisp **Manners
from Heaven, 1984** •593

I love a good dance ditty.
God, I love disco. I see no
problem admiring the Bee Gees
and being in The Sex Pistols.
Johnny Rotten **1998** •594

Barry White is the singer who turned
black soul music into a product akin
to soggy white blancmange. From Manila
to Macclesfield his voice could be heard,
grunting and gasping in a register of
emotions from A to B flat, invariably
expressing agitation at the prospect
of imminent sexual intercourse
and yet sounding as if somebody is
throttling the vocalist with a pillow.
Philip Norman •595

Village People are
about partying,
a twinkle in the
eye, and a bump
in the groin.
Victor Willis •596

They didn't look like humans.
They looked like foetuses. I felt
physically ill when I saw them on TV.

The ever-restrained *Julie Burchill* on Bay City Rollers •597

Freddie was always a star.
I remember him penniless
years ago coming round to
mine to bum a night's sleep
on the floor — and he'd act like
he was doing you a favour.

Queen's *Roger Taylor* 1974 •598

There was no way
people were ever
going to pay to
see Benny and
me performing.

Bjorn Ulvaeus Abba •599

We have to consider how we
would look now compared to
the memories people have of us.

Pop legends *Abba* explain why they turned down a
£650 million offer to perform again •600

A bit of Elvis, a bit of Bolan, a bit
of dub, a bit of rap, zap it through
a satellite dish and away we go.

Tony James Sigue Sigue Sputnik •601

You don't always choose the fifteen
minutes of fame that comes your way.

Hilary Lester **Renee of Renee and Renato** •602

All the bad publicity does toughen you up. The only way
you can deal with the criticism is by learning not to care.

Simon Le Bon **of Duran Duran** •603

We had a strange paranoia that we'd be
found out for the shallow charlatans we
really were. We really weren't good enough
to be adored by so many millions of people.

Tom Bailey **of The Thompson Twins. He's right** •604

I lay a £100,000 bet with anyone, any journalist, that there'll be a point in my career when I win an Oscar in Hollywood. There's no doubt about it.

Wendy James **of Transvision Vamp. Wish I'd taken the bet…** •605

In the 18-year old wake of David Bowie's *Pin Ups,* few artists have
been foolish enough to do a covers album. Duran Duran were the
last notable culprits with 1995's inexplicable *Thank You*; and now
Simple Minds have decided to come after them… Really, to call
this a turkey would be unfair to the birds who share the name.

John Harris **on Simple Minds' Neon Lights; in Q magazine, October 2001** •606

Jon was analytical; George intuitive. Jon was a
bit of a lad; George was as camp as Christmas.
And above all, George was the walking, talking,
made up, dressed up living embodiment of London's
underground nightlife. Jon thought the whole scene stank.
Dave Rimmer **on the contrasting lead members of Culture Club** •607

He was just starting out as a singer, he had the voice
but not the control, really. He was really mad keen on
rock music and the whole mythology of it. He loves it,
and he really deserves to be where he is today, even
though he was from Bromley and very middle class.
Rob Milne **on Billy Idol** •608

I wanted a name that would put us first in the
phonebook — or second, if you count Abba.
Martin Fry **ABC** •609

The essence of pop is brilliant songs.
The rest is sex, subversion, style
and humour. *Adam Ant* •610

You don't have to be a great musician
to make great records. You just have
to have a lot of good ideas. *Neneh Cherry* •611

Wham! worked like crazy to make people think they were lazy. Behind the sun tans lay the sweat and toil of self-improvement. *Dave Hill* •612

When you start measuring your achievements by records sold and size of gigs you're in trouble. Bananarama sold more records than The Supremes, but are they better? *Billy Bragg* 1996 •613

It's maybe something you wouldn't want to be caught playing with the car windows down.
David 'Kid' Jensen on **Chris De Burgh's Lady In Red** •614

He's at his best when marching fearlessly into yawning canyons of schlock, epitomised by his all-time end-of-the-party smoocher *Three Times a Lady*. When Lionel sang it, dozens of couples threw their arms around each other's necks and began to sway clumsily, as if Richie had pressed some biological Go button.
Adam Sweeting on the effect of Lionel Richie at a 1992 Town & Country gig •615

The first concert I went to without my mom was Tears For Fears. I was probably 13. All I remember was that I smoked a whole pack of cigarettes and promptly threw up everywhere. *Dido* 2001 •616

I was a veteran, before I was a teenager.
Michael Jackson •617

I come before you less as an icon of
pop and more as an icon of a generation.
Michael Jackson **speaking at the Oxford Union** •618

I feel like I'm Peter Pan, Methuselah, and a child.
Michael Jackson •619

I don't look at it as he is not the hottest thing any
more — I look at what he's done as a groundbreaking
artist who opened a lot of doors for black acts.
Michael Jackson is still amazing to me.
Missy Elliott •620

Michael is the wisest and at the same time most naive person I know.

Quincy Jones •621

Michael Jackson's album
was only called 'Bad' because
there wasn't enough room on
the sleeve for 'Pathetic'. *Prince* •622

Love Sexy, it has to be said, is a turgid collection of inconclusive riffs and weak melodies, decorated to distraction by harsh and flashy ornamentation.

David Toop on Prince's album Love Sexy, in The Sunday Times, May 1988 •623

Bambi with testosterone.

Owen Gleiberman **on Prince, in Entertainment Weekly** •624

He looks like a dwarf who's been dipped in a bucket of pubic hair.

Boy George on Prince •625

Kylie is an enigma really. I think that's part of her power. She's actually the opposite of Madonna — Madonna, we feel we know everything about. Kylie, we feel we know nothing about.

Neil Tennant **of the Pet Shop Boys, 2002** •626

I don't do anything to my backside. I work hard, I run around a lot and I dance when I have to. That's it.

Kylie **on her fitness regime after those infamous Spinning Around gold hotpants, 2002** •627

Boredom is thy enemy! Change
is as natural to me as breathing.

Kylie 2001 •628

I like seeing our records go up and Kylie
and Phil Collins go down. There's no point
moaning about it, you've got to get in there
and stamp them out. *Ian Brown* of The
Stone Roses 1990 •629

I loved Jordan. He was one of the greatest athletes of our time.
Mariah Carey pays a moving tribute to... er... the King of Jordan •630

The Celine Dion we know and love is
a handsome woman. That's not the
way I remember her from Eurovision.
Surely *Mr Wogan* isn't suggesting a bit of nip and tuck? •631

Don't want to hear my favourite
rapper doin' a love song. If I want
to hear something soft, I'll throw
on Luther Vandross. *Ice Cube* •632

187

I want our records to sell a million copies. I
want to make as much money as Phil Collins.
William Reid of The Jesus and Mary Chain 1993 •633

Shania 'Oh I must remember to buy some mutton' Twain once
performed at the Nobel Prize Peace Concert with Elton John and
Phil Collins. You probably remember that year. They had to wrestle
a Stanley knife off Nelson Mandela. *Mark Lamarr* •634

It's just like having all your fantasies
come true — partying for a living.

Fat Boy Slim •635

I'm not interested in just being today's pop
star. I want a career, like Stevie Wonder
or Sting or Queen. *Jason Kay* of Jamiroquai 1997 •636

A crippling affliction which leaves its victim unable to comprehend that no one
actually likes them, despite overwhelming evidence to the contrary. Named after
shamed dumper stalwart and ex Steps chipmunk Lisa Scott Lee, this terrifying
disease seems to be spreading through the pop wilderness like wildfire leaving
a number of has-beens desperately clinging onto the notion that they are still
popular, despite sales evidence to prove otherwise. Even the dedicated staff at
The Dumper have failed to find a cure, with Lisa Scott Lee herself still convinced
that her natural home is in the upper echelons of the chart.
popjustice.com define 'Lisa Scott-Lee Disease'. •637

Take That went to bed with coathangers in their mouths to wake up with smiles the next morning. East 17 went to bed with any young lady that was available to them. *Tom Watkins* **who managed both** •638

The worst thing you can do is try and be cool. Honesty is the best policy — just be a dick and people respect you for it. *Robbie Williams* •639

I show off — I'm a very good show off. It's what I do, it's what I'm good at. *Robbie Williams* •640

When people come out of rehab, they usually go to secondary rehab for another six months and then enter back into society gradually. But I came out and did Top Of The Pops straight away! *Robbie Williams* •641

I met Courtney Love and she said she'd like to sleep with me, but she couldn't cos of my 'pop-star thing'… so I said to her I couldn't sleep with her either — cos of her 'ugly thing'. *Robbie Williams* •642

When I first met him [David Beckham] I didn't know whether to shake his hand or lick his face. *Robbie Williams* •643

Noel's run out of other people's ideas. *Robbie Williams* **on Oasis's Noel Gallagher**•644

She's got a face like a satellite dish and ankles like my granny's. *Robbie Williams* **on British pop star Sophie Ellis Bextor** •645

We're the Spice Girls, yes indeed.
Just Girl Power is all we need.
The Spice Girls **master the art of rap in Spice World:**
The Movie (1997) •646

I don't think the Spice Girls are celebrated
as much as they should be. We championed
British pop worldwide. We toured everywhere
to sell-out crowds and I think there should
have been a reflection of that at February's
Brits anniversary. *Mel C* •647

We're becoming Spice Women now.
Mel C **on her new image •648**

'Okay, girls, that was
absolutely perfect without…
really being any good at all.'

Jools Holland **as the Spice Girls' musical director in their 1997 film Spice World •649**

Becoming a solo singer is like going from an eau
de toilette to a perfume. It's much more intense.
Geri Halliwell •650

She's the ultimate wannabe self-made pop star, a
pop dream. No matter where you live in the
world or how well you can sing, you can still be a
pop star. *John Robb* on the legacy of Geri Halliwell •651

Cowell: You sing like the Spice Girls.
Contestant: Thanks.
Cowell: Unfortunately, that wasn't a compliment.

From *Pop Idol* •652

I met someone the other night who's 28 years old, and
he hasn't worked a day since he left college because he's
pursuing a dream he'll never, ever realize: He thinks he's a
great singer. Actually, he's crap. But nobody has said to him,
'Why have you been wasting your time for eight years?'
Simon Cowell •653

The object of this competition is not to be mean to the losers but to find a winner. The process makes you mean because you get frustrated. Kids turn up unrehearsed, wearing the wrong clothes, singing out of tune and you can either say, 'Good job,' and patronize them or tell them the truth, and sometimes the truth is perceived as mean.

Simon Cowell on American Idol •654

Simon Cowell is the Antichrist, but there's room on this earth for the Antichrist.

David Byrne •655

I thought Pop Idol was really disappointing and full of freaks and geeks and fatties.

Marc Almond •656

Cee Lo is the black hip-hop Liberace.

Mark Burnett, Producer of US Reality TV show, The Voice •657

Where the hell is Australia anyway? *Britney Spears* •658

I love seeing all my Mexican fans from the North. *Britney Spears* •659

Britney would make a better prostitute than Christina. She's thicker. *Snoop Dogg* on the relative merits of La Spears and L'Aguilera •660

You are surrounded by people, each one more false than the other, always ready to step on you. Either you quickly learn to survive or you fail, you lose everything as quickly as you find success. *Christina Aguilera* •661

Britney and I show a little tummy and it's like, 'Oh My God.' But N'Sync or Backstreet Boys will do repeated pelvic thrusts to an audience of pre-pubescent girls and nobody says anything! *Christina Aguilera* •662

When popstars are 17 years old, the world and its pervy mother fancies them and says things like, 'Ooh I can't wait until they're 18 and I can get them bladdered down The Ram and do unspeakable acts to them'. Then the candles are blown out, the 18th birthday balloon pops and everyone realises they don't want to see said popstar's norks now they're 18 because it's all a bit 'sick'. See A-Teens, S Club Juniors, Charlotte Church, Richard Fleischeman *popjustice.com* explain the '17 year old itch' phenomenon •663

Oh dear, oh dear. Second-rate teeny acts (Samantha Mumba, a1, S Club 7) or people who promised never to trouble us again (Lulu, Lisa Stansfield, Yazz, Erasure) sing Motown songs badly. And what on earth the admirable Chris Rea — neither second-rate nor teen fodder — is doing here is something he should be discussing with his advisors right now; as he sacks them.

John Aizlewood on Motown Mania, by various artists, in Q magazine, March 2001 •664

I had my first snog with a boy under an electricity pylon. Which is quite dangerous, really. So don't do that, kids.

Jenny Frost of Atomic Kitten dispenses sage advice to the young •665

Me? An angel! Just ask my mum about that!

'Voice of an Angel' singer *Charlotte Church* on the limits of her angelic status •666

Everyone says I'm like the girl next door… Y'all must have really weird neighbours!

Kelly Clarkson •667

I'd die if I was Madonna. I'd die. God, what a horrible way to live. And Michael Jackson! To be so famous and to feel so isolated. I feel so bad for them. I don't know how it feels, and I hope it never happens to me.

Hollywood actress *Alicia Silverstone* •668

Sometimes I don't feel as if I am a person at all.
I'm just a collection of other people's ideas.
David Bowie •669

He was the Scarlet Pimpernel
in fabulous drag. *Mick Rock* on Bowie •670

I love girls. They're smashin'.
They're as good as blokes.
David Bowie 1972 •671

None of us exist. We're in the Twilight Zone. We'll all go to hell, 'cause we set ourselves up as Gods.
David Bowie 1972 •672

It's a movie that is so corrupt with a script that is so devious and insidious. It is the scariest movie ever written. You feel a total victim there, and you know someone's got the strings on you.
David Bowie **talking about Los Angeles** •673

Rock stars have taken over from the fake prophets of Jesus' time, spreading a phoney religion and getting paid for it.
David Bowie 1973 •674

I'm one of the world's actors, in the broadest sense of the word. I'm an exhibitionist. I like showing off. I'm a peacock.
David Bowie 1973 •675

It is Bowie, perhaps more than any other performer, who began the tyranny of style, image and media manipulation which has been the theme of pop music for the past ten years. *Mick Brown* •676

The first time I saw Ziggy Stardust it bowled me over. I was a journalist at the time, but that's when I decided I wanted to write songs and perform. *Steve Harley* 1974 •677

He is so dominating the teenage culture not only because he knows so many more things than his rivals, but because he understands how to exploit them to stay ahead, if only instinctively. *Michael Watts* 1976 •678

I have to pick a city with friction in it. It has to be a city that I don't know how it works. I've got to be at odds with it. As soon as I feel comfortable, I can't write in it any more.

David Bowie 1979 •679

He also provided the impetus for kids to dye their hair fantasy colours like blue, green, scarlet and purple — colours that human hair has never achieved unaided — to wear clothes based on *Flash Gordon* comics and 30s movies, to be exactly what they wanted to be and screw reality, Jack! *Charles Shaar Murray* •680

I had no melody, so I only sang the lines I'd written for five bars at a time. Having sung one line, I'd take a breath and do the same thing again, and so on to the end. I never knew the complete melody until I'd finished the song and played the whole the whole thing back.

David Bowie on Heroes •681

He said 'Can I change the lyrics?' I said,
'Of course, you're David Bowie; I live with
my mother. Of course you can change the lyrics.'
Luther Vandross on his collaboration with David Bowie •682

I feel like an actor when I'm onstage,
not a rock artist. It's not much of a
vocation, being a rock and roller.
David Bowie •683

I once asked John Lennon what
he thought of what I do. He said,
'It's great, but it's just rock and roll
with lipstick on.' *David Bowie* 1999 •684

I've been disappointed with some of my work,
but I do like an awful lot of it, I'm afraid. My
one problem is that I'm not very consistent.
David Bowie 1999 •685

Music is your own experience, your own thoughts, your
wisdom. If you don't live it, it won't come out of your horn.
They teach you there's a boundary line to music. But, man,
there's no boundary line to art. *Charlie Parker* 1955 •686

Life is like the car, and your art, or whatever
you produce, is the caravan. As long as the car's
in front of the caravan you can go places. The
other way around, you're not going anywhere.

Jarvis Cocker 2001 •687

A lot of our lyrics were obscure but not
unintelligent …thoughtful gibberish.

Ian McCulloch of Echo & The Bunnymen •688

It's like a novelist writing far out things. If it makes a
point and makes sense, then people like to read that.
But if it's off in left field and goes over the edge, you
lose it. The same with musical talent, I think.
Johnny Cash •689

An artist's duty is rather to stay open-minded and in a state
where he can receive information and inspiration. You
always have to be ready for that little artistic Epiphany.
Nick Cave •690

Rock 'n' roll, man, it changed my life. It was like the Voice of America, the real America coming into your home. It was the liberating thing, the out. Once I had the guitar, I had the key to the highway. *Bruce Springsteen* 1978 •691

The message in the records is, just follow your heart, as corny as that may sound. There are people trying to hold onto the things they believe in, but it's all very difficult.
Bruce Springsteen 1978 •692

What's wrong with sentimental? Sentimental means you love, you care, you like stuff. The thing is, we're frightened to be sentimental. *Paul McCartney* 1983 •693

I like a spirituality with a God that knows how to take his girl to the dance club, dance all night, have a little drink, kiss the kid when they come back in and go to sleep. God doesn't need a chauffeur. *Jeff Buckley* 1994 •694

My idea of heaven is a place where the Tyne meets the Delta, where folk music meets the blues. *Mark Knopfler*
Mojo, 1986 •695

I am a perfectionist. Some even claim that I'm a terrorist, a dictator and they're right. But I'm also talented and I know when I create something great.
Lou Reed 1998 •696

Rebellion, love, hate, sex, denial: all these will
still be here when we're done. I like to stick to
the old standbys in my songs. *Paul Westerberg* of The
Replacements 1993 •697

That's why I do this music business thing, it's
communication with people without having the
extreme inconvenience of actually phoning anybody up.
Morrissey •698

Immortality doesn't bother me. If people
have forgotten about *I Don't Like Mondays*
two weeks from now, no problem. *Bob Geldof* 1979 •699

Everyone goes on about the idea of the sensitive
artist, but for me that's all bollocks. I can't stand
the idea of being a sad, lonely bedside poet
I'd much rather be perceived as loud and arrogant.
Damon Albarn of Blur 1997 •700

It's always a Catch-22 situation. They hate
you if you're the same, and they hate you
if you're different. *Eddie Van Halen* •701

Artists everywhere steal mercilessly
all the time and I think this is healthy.
Peter Gabriel 1992 •702

I'm not plagued, I'm strictly a loner.
I don't have any friends. I like to be
on my own best of all. *Scott Walker*
Melody Maker, 1966 •703

People sometimes ask me if I'm happy, and I tell them to fuck off.
Thom Yorke **of Radiohead 1995 •704**

I hate art. I can't stand it. It's treating something
that's supposed to be good as precious. But it
ain't precious. Anyone can make a record.
John Lydon •705

We can all make music individually.
But we are smart enough to know that
the music we make together is far better.
Peter Buck **of REM on the band ethic •706**

Anybody that forms a group, writes songs
and releases records and says they don't
care if people like them are complete liars.
James Dean Bradfield **of the Manic Street Preachers 2001 •707**

Words aren't the salad dressing on the meal of music.
Words are the first thing for me. I like having a finished lyric
that I'm pleased with, and letting the music follow from there.
Mike Scott **of The Waterboys** •708

Originally, the function of songs was devotional, I think.
Then in the balladeering centuries, they became a vehicle for the
spreading of information, stories and opinions. Now in the 20th century
they become a way of making money and achieving fame. I think the
other two purposes are much better. *Mike Scott* **of The Waterboys** •709

A record doesn't detail a person's changes.
If I make a record, that's it. It doesn't affect how
I live. And it isn't how I live. It doesn't affect my
life, and my life doesn't affect it. What can you
say on 40 minutes of wax? *Van Morrison* 1973 •710

Just because the songs are about reality, there's no reason
for music to be boring or depressing. Music is about uplifting
people, you know? *Shane MacGowan* **ex-Pogues 1995** •711

It's a great song, it really is.
I wish I could remember it.

Shane MacGowan **on Fairytale of New York** •712

The band wanted to know why I wrote miserable songs all the time. I hadn't even noticed.
Natalie Merchant of 10,000 Maniacs •713

Our music is made from natural impulses. There's no cynical exploitation.
Ed Simons of The Chemical Brothers •714

I'm not a moody songwriter. I don't need to go to the Caribbean to produce. It's a gift from God, it just comes. *Smokey Robinson* •715

Berry Gordy taught me how to make my songs be a story, with a beginning, a middle, an end and a theme.
Smokey Robinson •716

My songs are my kids and some of them stay with me. Some others I have to send out, out to the war. It might even sound naive, but that's just the way it is.
Thom Yorke of Radiohead 2000 •717

I've always liked a tinge of melancholy in songs, and I find
that even on a perfect day anxieties are always close.
Tim Finn of Crowded House •718

Going to a 7-eleven in the middle of the night and
hearing the clerk whistling one of my songs — that's
my idea of a great cover version. *Warren Zevon* 2000 •719

The verses are the blues,
the chorus is the gospel.
Bruce Springsteen 2002 •720

I've always held the song in high regard because
songs have got me through so many sinks of dishes
and so many humiliating courting events.
Leonard Cohen 1998 •721

Songs do have the power to change things. Music
has changed my life, it has changed your life, it
has changed everyone's lives. *Christy Moore* 2006 •722

It's a marvellous feeling when someone says
'I want to do this song of yours' because
they've connected to it. That's what I'm after.
Mary Chapin Carpenter •723

You shouldn't have to worry
about where you come from.
We just want to get good
music back on the charts.
Chris Martin of Coldplay 2001 •724

We knew we needed a 'chant' song, because
the Bay City Rollers had 'Saturday Night'.
Johnny Ramone **discussing the origins of Blitzkrieg Bop** 2001 •725

The words just came into my head: 'she packed
my bags last night, pre-flight. Zero hour is 9 a.m.'
I remember jumping out of the car and running into
my parents house, shouting, please don't anyone talk
to me until I've written this down. *Bernie Taupin* **on writing**
Rocket Man •726

I don't know why I bother really,
because people don't listen to lyrics
in rock 'n' roll records too much.
Lou Reed 1989 •727

My vocal style I haven't tried to copy from anyone. It just
developed until it became the girlish whine it is today.
Robert Plant •728

> I can recall copying the sound of the
> coalman who used to come round.
> *Eric Burdon* of The Animals •729

If God had nuh given me a song to sing,
I wouldn't have a song to sing. The
song comes from God, all the time.
Bob Marley •730

> Reggae has to be inside you…
> Reggae music is simple, all the while…
> Cannot be taught, that's a fact.
> *Bob Marley* Melody Maker, 1976 •731

I've got a few demons, but I manage to co-exist with
'em. That's what makes you crazy, that's what makes
me play my guitar the way I play it sometimes.
Neil Young •732

> *Heart of Gold* put me in the middle of the road. Travelling
> there soon became a bore so I headed for the ditch. A
> rougher ride, but I saw more interesting people there.
> *Neil Young* •733

I play the way I do because it allows me
to come up with the sickest sounds possible.
That's the point now isn't it? *Jeff Beck* •734

Andy Warhol once said to me, years ago, that I
was to music what he was to the visual arts. You
can't define it. But it's all happening the way he
said it would. The man's amazing. ***Lou Reed*** 1974 •735

Lou learned a lot from Andy, mainly about becoming a
successful public personality by selling your own private
quirks to an audience greedy for more and more geeks.
Lester Bangs **on Andy Warhol's influence on Lou Reed** (1975) •736

Lou Reed has always epitomised New York for fellow
media observers, both in his lifestyle and his art.
The chronicler of the shadow world, the deviants,
the drug limbo, the concrete jungle, he is
the poet laureate of that city. *Mick Rock* 1972 •737

You're always in the desert looking for an oasis,
and all that's out there with you is the piano, this big
black beast with eighty-eight teeth. *Billy Joel* •738

I think Lou writes in a much more detached manner
from me. Lou's the kind of guy who sits back and watches
what's going on and takes notes… he's a natural journalist.
He's almost become a kind of musical Woody Allen…
David Bowie •739

I've still got edge in my music, hopefully
always will have — and if my music ever got
as laid back as Eric Clapton's I'd pack it in.
Or shoot myself. *Paul Weller* •740

John Fogerty was an Old
Testament, shaggy-haired prophet.

Bruce Springsteen on John Fogerty of Creedance Clearwater Revival •741

Some people are
very cerebral and
can dream a little.
We do manual labour.

Jay Farrar of Son Volt, 1995 •742

211

We took from jazz, old-fashioned rock 'n' roll,
the classics. We were musical magpies.
Jon Lord of Deep Purple •743

We just did our own thing: a combination
of rock 'n' roll, Fellini, game-show host,
corn and mysticism. *Fred Schneider* B-52's •744

It is an iron law of pop music that if you go away
for too long, you come back sounding like the
people who've ripped you off in the interim.
Ben Thompson on Television's return in 1992 •745

Waits is an originator without being the least bit original.
He was the first in a long line of white spade urban
rock 'n' roll poets who chose to romanticise the sleazy side
of the tracks. This approach had been done to death in the
literature of the Beat Generation, but Waits was the first to
successfully bring it above ground on vinyl.
Terri A. Huggins •746

I'm what they used to call a troubadour.
What I do for a living is to get people to
feeling good. *Willie Nelson* •747

The best country music is incredibly simple, yet very poignant and moving.

Emmylou Harris •748

You've got to have smelled a lot of mule manure before you can sing like a hillbilly.
Hank Williams *quoted by* Tony Palmer in 1976 •749

It is something powerful and mysterious arising from the no-hope towns and the forgotten enclaves of the West and the tin tabernacles and back porches of the hills — from the sill-beating heart of old, weird America.

Brian Hinton, author of South By South-West, on the unifying spirit of country music •750

If you are a songwriter, did anyone ask you if you wanted to spend the rest of your career modifying your lyric content to suit the spiritual needs of an imaginary eleven-year-old?
Frank Zappa The Real Frank Zappa Book 1989 •751

213

For a start, I've got to be out of my head to write.
Shane MacGowan **of The Pogues** 1989 •752

It's easier to write about things
that are falling apart than things
that are beautiful and perfect. *Beck* 1996 •753

It's actually really hard to write a
happy song without sounding corny.
Carl Bell **of Fuel** 2001 •754

Listen, the easiest way to get laid
by a girl, or get rid of her, is to
write a song about her. *David Crosby* 1970's •755

I try to bring back some intelligence to music,
instead of just four chords and dumb lyrics.
I'll match the power of my ballads with anything
Nirvana are doing. *Barry Manilow* •756

The trick of writing is to make it sound
like it's all happening for the first time.
Tim Buckley •757

People think it's glamorous, songwriting, but
this is what it's really about, walking around
singing to yourself like a loony.
Elvis Costello 1995 •758

We're the best of friends, but
always fighting. It was there
right from the beginning. There
has to be creative tension.
Stewart Copeland of Police, 1985 •759

It's a physical, emotional, and intellectual process.
Not to sound too high falutin' about it, but it's an
immediate process that involves all my faculties.
It's an interplay between the conscious
and subconscious. *Moby* 2000 •760

Pete, as far as writing songs goes and coming up with
general basic ideas, he's fantastic. But Pete Townshend
is not The Who. And I think the first person to admit that
will be Pete Townshend. And you've got to realise that.
The Who is four people. *Roger Daltrey* 1976 •761

I write a song because I am deeply moved to write a song. It's a very simple process in that way.
Adam Duritz of Counting Crows 1996 •762

To me, songwriting is almost like stamp collecting — except that I collect fragments of other peoples lives.

David Gedge of The Wedding Present 1993 •763

I tried to write these meaningful songs and always, the whole time, I would come back to monkeys and chickens and frogs. *Chris Balew* of The Presidents of The United States 1995 •764

When I'm writing my songs, I get to parts of me I've hidden for so long. And it's a liberating place to be.
Tori Amos 1996 •765

I write for myself and I try to make it something I would listen to. I operate under the idea that I'm not unusual. And if I try to do it really well for myself, other people can relate to it, too. But I don't really know how to write for other people so I can't do that. *Lou Reed* 1998 •766

I've written most of my best songs driving
on a long journey scribbling lyrics on
cigarette packets whilst steering. *Neil Young* •767

Those first five or six songs that I wrote, I
was just taking notes at a fantastic rock concert
that was going on inside my head. And once
I had written the songs, I had to sing them.

Jim Morrison •768

I always make sure I have a guitar around. I might suddenly get
an idea for a song. I don't sit around saying: now I'm going to
write a song. they come to me. I firmly believe they're floating
through the room right now. You don't create them, you find them.
Keith Richards •769

Whenever I don't know what to write about,
I just close my eyes and think of Essex.
Damon Albarn in Blah Blah Blah magazine,1996 •770

I don't think songwriters listen to themselves talk.
They fall into rock cliches. That's what I try to avoid.
Aimee Mann •771

I've never been interested in writing pop songs.
I don't consider myself part of pop music at all.
Lou Reed •772

I write pop songs. But I think it is sprinkled
with a lot of counter-culture references.
It ranged from rap to hip hop to trip hop,
house, drum and bass, and experimental
and improv and jazz. *Nelly Furtado* •773

I guess I just lucked out that I like writing songs
and people like my songs. That's the catch.
You do what you like and that's fine, but if no
one else likes it, eventually, you run out of steam.
Wayne Coyne of The Flaming Lips 1999 •774

When you stop putting yourself on the line, and you don't touch your own heart, how do you expect to touch other people?

Tori Amos •775

Fame threw me for a loop at first. I learned how to swim with it and turned it around. So you can just throw it in the closet and pick it up when you need it.

Bob Dylan •776

The songs are insanely honest, not meanin' to twist any head, and written only for the reason that I myself, me alone wanted and needed to write them.

Bob Dylan 1964 •777

In writing songs I've learned as much from Cezanne as I have from Woody Guthrie.

Bob Dylan quoted in Behind The Shades, by Clinton Heylin, 1991 •778

The folk music scene had been like a paradise
that I had to leave, like Adam had to leave the
garden. It was just too perfect. *Bob Dylan* Chronicles •779

An easy way out would be to say, 'yes, it's all
behind me, that's it and there's no more.' But
you want to say that there might be a small
chance that something up there will surpass
whatever you did. Everybody works in the
shadow of what they've previously done.
But you have to overcome that.
Bob Dylan 1989 •780

There was a presence in the room that couldn't
have been anybody but Jesus. I truly had a born-
again experience, if you want to call it that.
Jesus put his hand on me. It was a physical
thing. I felt it. I felt it all over me. I felt my
whole body tremble. The glory of the Lord
knocked me down and picked me up.
Bob Dylan on his experience in a Tuscon
hotel room, November 1978 •782

I went over my whole life. I went
over my whole childhood. I didn't
talk to anyone for a week after
Elvis died. If it wasn't for Elvis
and Hank Williams, I wouldn't
be doing what I do today.
Bob Dylan 1978 •781

The closest I ever got to the sound
I hear in my mind was on individual
bands in the *Blonde on Blonde*
album. It's that thin, that wild
mercury sound. It's metallic and
bright gold, with whatever that
conjures up. That's my
particular sound.
Bob Dylan 1978 •783

I knew that when I got into folk music it was more of a serious type thing. The songs were filled with more despair, more sadness, more triumph, more faith in the supernatural, much deeper feelings… life is full of complexities, and rock and roll didn't reflect that. *Bob Dylan* •784

Mr Hammond asked me if I wanted to sing any of them over again and I said no. I can't see myself singing the same song twice in a row. That's terrible. **Bob Dylan on recording his debut album in 1961** •785

I was completely taken over by him. He was like a guide. *Bob Dylan on Woody Guthrie* •786

What's money? A man is a success if he gets up in the morning and gets to bed at night and in between he does what he wants to. *Bob Dylan* •787

I like those people who come to see me now. They're not aware of my early days, but I'm glad of that. It lifts that burden of responsibility, of having to play everything exactly like it was on some certain record. I can't do that. Which way the wind is blowing, they're going to come out different every time. *Bob Dylan* 1998 •788

If I had a good quote, I'd be wearing it.

Bob Dylan in reply to a French journalist who asked for 'a good quote',
quoted in The Times, July 1981 •789

I think that's just another word for a washed-up has-been.

Bob Dylan on being an 'Icon' •790

Actually, I never liked Dylan's kind
of music before, I always thought
he sounded like Yogi Bear.
Mick Ronson •791

I did Dylan, and he fucked me over. I hate that guy. That was the most
miserable session, too. I did a really good job on it, and he kept my playing on there even when the advance copies went to the record company.
Then at the last moment he took it off because he said it sounded too
much like Guns n' Roses. Why did he call me, y'know?
Slash 1991 •792

This voice was like broken glass, like spitting.
The words were like arrows, being shot straight
into the heart of the establishment. That was what
made me realise what the words of a song could do.
Bernie Taupin on hearing The Times They Are A Changin', 1964 •793

223

Dylan was, like many young people who admired him,
a disturbed, unconventional, rebellious and confused internal
exile from affluence he could have had, but did not want.
Lawrence Goldman Studies on the Left, 1968 •794

He was rarely tender, and seldom reached out
to anticipate another's needs, though occasionally
he would exhibit a sudden concern for another
outlaw, hitchhiker, or bum, and got out of
his way to see them looked after.
Joan Baez 1988 •795

I had never been on a professional, big-time session with studio musicians.
I didn't know anything. I liked the songs. If you'd been there, you would have
seen it was a very disorganised, weird scene. Since then I've played on millions
of sessions and I realise how really weird that Dylan session was.
Mike Bloomfield 1968 •796

The Chimes of Freedom shows that his love of
the majestic, big, epic type of material is all but
a permanent side of Bob Dylan. How many artists
would come right out and say they are singing for
'every hung-up person in the whole wide universe'?
John Landau in Crawdaddy •797

By today's standards it wasn't very loud, but by those standards of the day was the loudest thing anybody had ever heard... there were arguments between people sitting next to each other. Some people were booing, some people were cheering.

Joe Boyd on Dylan's famous first electric performance at Newport •798

Highway 61 re-invented rock 'n' roll in a way perhaps only half a dozen albums have done in the 40 year history of the art.

Clinton Heylin in Behind The Shades 1991 •799

Dylan was 25. In just five years he had transformed popular music beyond recognition, making rock 'n' roll capable of saying a great deal more than just Awopbopaloobop, and had been vilified, glorified, even deified for his trouble.

Clinton Heylin in Behind The Shades 1991 •800

Bob's music really is dependent on catching the moment — they're like snapshots, Polaroids. The first take is gonna be better even if it's got some wrong notes.

Rob Stoner Dylan's bass player on the Desire album •801

The nature of the artist is that he keeps going. The paradox of the audience is that we love him for this, and yet we want him to stop and stay in the place where he touched us last, or most.

Paul Williams in Bob Dylan, Performing Artist 1990 •802

Dylan to me is the perfect symbol of the anti-artist in our society. He is against everything — the last resort of someone who doesn't really want to change the world… Dylan's songs accept the world as it is.

Ewan MacColl on Bob Dylan, Melody Maker, 1965 •803

Bob Dylan's music
is the greatest music
ever written, to me.
The man says it all,
exactly the right way.
Incredibly powerful.
You don't get no
more intense.

Bruce Springsteen 1980 •804

If there's a problem, you have to go out and solve it.

Bob Geldof •805

No, Prime Minister, nothing
is as simple as dying.

Bob Geldof remonstrates with Margaret Thatcher •806

People are dying NOW.
Give us the money NOW.
Give me the money now.

Geldof at Live Aid •807

Fuck the address, just give
the phone... here's the number...
Geldof at Live Aid, oft misquoted as
'give us yer fucking money...' •808

I've just realized that today is the best day
of my life. Now I'm going home to sleep.
Geldof at Live Aid •809

Not to be immodest, but the first one was perfect in almost
every sense… Artistically, people seemed to up the ante,
and the performances were pretty great across the board.
Huge amounts of money were raised, not a penny lost, and
politically it elevated the issue onto the global table. The
whole thing just worked, unbelievably. *Geldof* at Live Aid •810

One can have great concern for the people
of Ethiopia, but it's another thing to inflict
daily torture on the people of England.
Morrissey on the Band Aid song •811

Edge can say more about the
struggle in El Salvador with his
guitar than the written word.
Bono •812

This musical thing been here since America
been here. This is trial and tribulation music.
Mahalia Jackson **gospel singer and civil rights
activist, in Time magazine, 1968** •813

God never made no difference between black,
white, blue, pink or green. People is people, y'know.
Bob Marley •814

Here was this Third World superstar emerging,
an individual against the system with an incredible
look: this was the first time you had seen anyone
looking like that, other than Jimi Hendrix. And Bob
had that power about him and incredible lyrics.
Chris Blackwell **on Bob Marley** •815

When I left school there was nothing to do except field work;
hard, hard labour. I didn't fancy that. So I started playing dominoes.
Through dominoes I practised my mind and learned to read the
minds of others. This has proved eternally useful to me.
Jamaican reggae master, *Lee "Scratch" Perry* •816

I've never bought a Bob Dylan record.
A singing poet? It just bores me to tears.

Simon Cowell **shows the breadth of his attention span** •817

We're tired of beating our head against the wall
And working for someone else.
We're people, we're like the birds and the bees
But we'd rather die on our feet than keep living on our knees.

James Brown **Say It Loud, I'm Black and I'm Proud,
(with Alfred Ellis) (1969)** •818

Justice costs. It's for people who
can really afford justice. So music fills
the place of working man's justice.

Ben Harper •819

FRANKIE SAY ARM THE UNEMPLOYED

Frankie Goes To Hollywood T-shirt slogan, a riff
on their Frankie Says Relax motto •820

We're not preachers, and we're not leaders.
Our fans see us as people who are saying
exactly what they'd like to say in our position.
Simon Friend of The Levellers •821

You've got to walk it like you talk it, or else
you're just exploiting it, don't you think?
It's hard to find a way to do that.
Billy Bragg •822

I don't think people are converted to socialism
by eye contact with me. *Billy Bragg* 1997 •823

A septic isle — grey, boring, shitty.
The inner city kids weren't alright.

Ian Dury **on 1970s Britain •824**

Me mam gets £70 a week as a pensioner and she had
to pay £120 a year to watch people on TV doing their
fuckinghouses up. You can see that anywhere. If you
want to see fucking builders, just look out the window.

Mark E Smith **of The Fall •825**

It's the easiest thing in the world to write a song
saying "America is evil." When Jarvis Cocker sings
"Cunts are running the world," I think, "Here we go,
what have you ever done? Fucking fiddled with your
arse in front of Michael Jackson…"

Nicky Wire **of Manic Street Preachers •826**

There were highly placed people in Her Majesty's government who saw us as enemies of the state. They decided to plot the downfall of the Stones.

Marianne Faithfull on pop and political conspiracy •827

As long as I'm attacked by the KGB and the CIA, then I'm probably on the right track.

Joan Baez 1988 •828

I'm interested in anything about revolt, disorder, chaos, especially activity that appears to have no meaning. It seems to me to be the road toward freedom.

Jim Morrison Time magazine, 1968 •829

If I'm more of an influence to your son
as a rapper than you are as a father...
you got to look at yourself as a parent.

Ice Cube **Rolling Stone, 1994** •830

Basically, the Bible was the first fucking police force.

Shaun Ryder, **no stranger to the law** •831

I still don't know who the fuck I am. I know what I don't
believe in. I know what I've rejected. But I don't know
what I do believe in. *Trent Reznor* **of Nine Inch Nails (1995)** •832

Freedom's just another word for nothing left to lose.
Kris Kristofferson **Me and Bobby McGhee (1969)** •833

236

As a revolutionary and leader of
people at the barricades, I failed.
But as a person who inwardly revolts
all the time, I'm a raging success.

Roy Harper •834

If you don't confront censorship, then the music of confrontational artists will be silenced.

Tom Morello of Rage Against The Machine, 1993 •835

When you get your ass kicked that hard, it makes
you go to the innermost depths of what you are all
about as a human being. Now, maybe most people
have not been kicked that hard, but it's still in
everybody, and this music rings a bell that you
can hear throughout the fucking world.
Quincy Jones talking about the blues.
Rolling Stone, 1976 •836

We always set out to make records about ideas and attitudes that are important and real: the band we never had when we were growing up.

Richie Edwards of Manic Street Preachers •837

We never thought of it as being any great statement — it was just the way Black Flag did things.

Greg Ginn •838

Music has ceased to belong to the young… the rock rebel is defunct. He's meaningless.

Sting Smash Hits, 1982 •839

238

I never tackled an issue, social, political
or otherwise, unless there was a metaphor
in which to dress it up. I was never into
writing propaganda or polemic.
Sting 2000 •840

If ever I would stop thinking about music and politics
I would tell you that music is the expression of emotion
and that politics is merely the decoy of perception.
The Disposable Heroes of Hiphoprisy
Music and Politics (1992) from the album
Hypocrasy Is the Greatest Luxury •841

I want to do anything I can to promote AIDS education,
awareness, prevention — whatever. I think because I'm
a celebrity, a public person, I have a real responsibility
to be a spokesperson. Next to Hitler, AIDS is the worst
thing to happen to the 20th century. *Madonna* •842

I have this kinda naive idea that the world should be a different place than it is right now, and I'd like to be involved in changing it by trying to understand more and be honest about my understanding.
Moby 1999 •843

There's no point in being subversive in rock anymore, there's no way you can be — unless you ram a stick of dynamite up your ass. *Kurt Cobain* of Nirvana 1992 •844

I want someone to rob a bank in the name of Green Day. I want them to make masks of our faces and rob a fucking bank.
Billie Joe Armstrong of Green Day 1997 •845

If this was a slightly more primitive time I would already be burning at the stake. I expect there is still time for that. *Morrissey* 1989 •846

These days, everyone wants John Lennon's sunglasses, accent and swagger, but no one is prepared to take their clothes off and stand naked like he did in his songs. Putting your head over the parapet means something completely different these days, but it's still a big part of what rock and roll is all about for me. You have to use your celebrity, negotiate your position and be aware that celebrity can diminish a cause as much as illuminate it. *Bono* 2000 •847

Neil Tennant: As if people think, 'oh, we think war's fantastic, actually, but I've now changed my mind because John Lennon's told me peace is a good thing.'
Chris Lowe: He's enough to make you want to go to war, John Lennon.
The Pet Shop Boys on Lennon's legacy •848

Everything went downhill from the moment McDonald's was given a license to invade England… To me, it was like the outbreak of war and I couldn't understand why English troops weren't retaliating. *Morrissey* **The Guardian, 1994** •849

As rock stars we witnessed the flowering of a new consciousness founded on sex, drugs, rock and the renunciation of Americana.
John Phillips **of the Mamas and Papas** •850

On (the day of the attack) the victims were American. But the horrible scenes that we're witnessed on TV this week are regular occurrences in other places around the globe. And too often, violence like this has been meted out by our own country and its client states. We should stand together against this type of violence in all its forms, whenever it happens, whether it is done in the name of religious fanaticism, or in the name of our own domestic elite.
Tom Morello **of Rage Against The Machine, on 9/11** •851

I don't like you. I don't like your boss. I don't like what you did. Thank you.

Bruce Springsteen **declines an audience with Oliver North, offered via North's secretary in 1988** •852

The guy in 'Born In The USA' wants to strip away that mythic America which was Reagan's image of America. He wants to find something real and connecting. He's looking for a home in his country. *Bruce Springsteen* 1987 •853

I wouldn't say a single word to them, I would listen to what they have to say and that's what no one did.
Marilyn Manson when asked what he would say to the kids in Columbine, where a massacre was enacted and people pointed the finger at his influence •854

Anybody intelligent enough to realize what America is, is not going to sit around and do nothing about it. They're going to be the same way that I am. They're going to be the same way our fans are. They're going to be pissed.
Marilyn Manson •855

I was waiting for some young singer to come along, to write these songs and stand up. I waited a long time.
Neil Young is, not unreasonably, disappointed with the younger generation's failure to register their disapproval of the Bush regime •856

All the great political music was made
at the height of political confrontations

Billy Bragg •857

You can't trust politicians. It doesn't matter
who makes a political speech. It's all lies…
and it applies to any rock star who wants
to make a political speech as well.

Bob Geldof •858

Walking through the doors at 10 Downing Street,
not as a plumber, but an invited guest. I'm glad
I did it to have a look, but in terms of New Labour,
I recognise now that we were conned. We thought
Tony Blair was John F. Kennedy, when in fact he
was John Major with a better PR team.

Noel Gallagher 2001 •859

Every time I come back to Britain from elsewhere I get pissed off. It's the civil liberties thing. Even when people are partying on the Berlin Wall, you can't do it near the M25. *Will* of The Shamen, 1990 •860

When you realize that all governments fail at one time or another, it takes the shine off of democracy and all of its speeches and policies. You realize it's all an empty she-bang.

Joe Strummer 2001 •861

Most governments don't last as long as this band.
Peter Buck of R.E.M. 1998 •862

Left wing, chicken wing, it don't make no difference to me.

Woody Guthrie •863

The lame part of the Sixties was the political part, the social part. The real part was the spiritual part.
Jerry Garcia •864

Every rebellion is co-opted and in 50 years is seen as a natural progression from what came before.
Stephen Malkmus of Pavement, 1994 •865

Messages become a drag like preaching. I think one of the worst possible beliefs is that pop stars know more about life than anyone else.

Nick Mason of Pink Floyd •866

● *From the Indulgent..*

If you looked up the word 'pretentious' in
the dictionary, you could possibly see a
picture of Emerson, Lake and Palmer.
Carl Palmer •867

Copeland heard my arrangement of Hoe-down and
he was knocked out by it… We'd altered it with a
very finely dotted quaver because it didn't swing
the other way. *Keith Emerson* •868

It's not art in the same
way as painting a picture.

Keith Emerson Oh really, Keith? How f***ing enlightening •869

Jazz is an ocean. Rock 'n' roll is a
swimming pool. I hang out on a lake.
Carlos Santana •870

If art were to redeem man, it could do so only
by saving him from the seriousness of life, and
restoring him to an unexpected boyishness.
John Lennon •871

249

People described her voice as everything from
eerie to bland and smooth, to wind in a drainpipe,
to an IBM computer with a Garbo accent.
Andy Warhol on Nico •872

Yes and Genesis are as exciting as a used Kleenex.

Nick Lowe •873

Like a foul alignment of all the black planets, this collection of 95-97 material
culled from the Keys to Ascension I and II albums, saw all the important members
of Yes […] reunited to wreak havoc on the world. Chords are played at random,
tunes change tempo for no other reason than that is what happens in symphonies
and tracks are long just for longness's sake… The fact that they had a hit single as
recently as 15 years ago should serve as a warning to us all that this sort of thing
could strike at any moment. *David Quantick* reviews Yes's album Keys to the Studio
in Q Magazine, September 2001 •874

Our music has depth, and attempts philosophical thought
and meaning with discussions of infinity, eternity and
mortality. There is a line which people cross that turns
it into some magical, mystical realm, for which I don't
claim responsibility and don't hold any great truck with.
Dave Gilmour of Pink Floyd •875

Above all, Roxy Music is a state of mind. Hollywood movies
meets English art school, with a little Schopenhauer thrown in,
both in the lyrics I write and the way we look. Of course, that allows
for all kinds of possibilities. I am, you might say, a collagiste.
Bryan Ferry 1975. •876

He wanted to combine the fastidiousness of art with the sweat
of rock 'n' roll music. He explains this in a set speech, then
apologises for having delivered it. *Philip Norman*
on Bryan Ferry •877

Ambient Music must be able to accommodate many
levels of listening attention without enforcing one in
particular; it must be as ignorable as it is interesting.
Brian Eno **sleevenotes to Music For Airports, 1979** •878

Analysis is like a lobotomy. Who wants
to have all their edges shaved off? *David Byrne* •879

To sing is to love and to affirm, to fly and
soar, to coast into the hearts of the people
who listen, to tell them that life is to live,
that love is there, that nothing is a promise,
but that beauty exists, and must be hunted
for and found. *Joan Baez* **Daybreak, 'Singing',1970** •880

Please don't write that we eat.
We don't want the fans to think that we eat.
***Robin Guthrie* of The Cocteau Twins** •881

The greatest conflicts
are not between two
people but between one
person and himself.

Garth Brooks •882

Am I a fruitcake? I don't know.
Perception is reality. What you see
me as in your world is what I am; it
doesn't matter what I am. *Macy
Gray* •883

I like our name because its so easy to spell.
It's real authentic. It's pop art, in a sense.
***Ric Ocasek* of The Cars** •884

Supernature is a story of good and evil. What I want
to say to people is to leave each thing in its proper
place, otherwise the monsters will be coming. *Cerrone* •885

I hope to refine music, study it, try to find some area
that I can unlock. I don't quite know how to explain it
but it's there. These can't be the only notes in the world,
there's got to be other notes some place, in some
dimension, between the cracks on the piano keys.
Marvin Gaye •886

Jesus was a Capricorn and I'm a Capricorn. Jesus was a carpenter
and I was a carpenter. I've spent years trying to draw attention to
the similarities between myself and Jesus… Usually the response
is that people move to another part of the pub.

A tongue-in-cheek Jim Reid (of the Jesus and Mary Chain) •887

My records are built like a
Wagnerian opera; they start
simply and they end with dynamic
force, meaning and purpose. *Phil Spector* •888

We play the machines, but the machines also play us.

Ralf Hutter of Kraftwerk •889

I had a shrink when I was in the nuthouse, and he gave me one good rule that's stuck with me. He said, 'Before you do anything, ask yourself; am I going to get away with it?'

Iggy Pop •890

I'm not a tortured artist, and there's nothing really wrong with me. I just had a bad time for a while.

Elliott Smith 2001 •891

● *Through the delusional...*

God made me — but
I created the myth. *James Brown* •892

I've outdone anyone you can name — Mozart,
Beethoven, Bach, Strauss. Irving Berlin, he
wrote 1,001 tunes. I wrote 5,500. **James Brown** •893

I think I'm right on the threshold of bursting through. I feel
I'm as good as Beethoven or any of the greats. I don't compare
myself to Beethoven, I must make that clear. I just think that
I'm capable of all that he was capable of. ***Marvin Gaye*** 1973 •894

I'm an artist and that means I can
be as egotistical as I want to be.
Lou Reed 1998 •895

My style of music is so far out in its own
field that I don't even want to explain it.
It's gone beyond the point where I can
communicate it on a verbal level.
Iggy Pop 1972 •896

How can you consider flower power outdated?
The essence of my lyrics is the desire for peace
and harmony. That's all anyone has ever wanted.
How could it become outdated? *Robert Plant* •897

Salvador Dali showed me
that everything was possible.
Edgar Froese of Tangerine Dream •898

I could sing like Caruso if I wanted to,
but he's already done it. *Tom Waits* •899

My art is more important to me than just
being remembered as the person who got
five million to be sponsored by Coca-Cola.
Terence Trent D'Arby •900

I happen to believe I'm a genius. As time proves
me right, I'm becoming less and less afraid to say so.
Terence Trent D'Arby 1988 •901

Art is born inside someone and comes out into something
that you can experience and that's all it is. There's no
difference between Beethoven and Johnny Rotten.
There's no difference between Beethoven and me.
Adam Duritz of Counting Crows, 1998. •902

I believe our purpose
is to inspire and guide
the human race. *Sinead O'Connor*
**on the nature of pop music,
The Independent, 1991** •903

I could not take the brunt of standing in the light of my own work.
There was a Faustian bargain I could not make. I could have you mock
me for wearing funny clothes, that I could deal with. But I couldn't deal
with actually standing in the light of my own musical power. *Billy Corgan* •904

I think we're relevant, we're important!
We're exciting, mind expanding!

Ian Brown **of The Stone Roses** •905

We're the most important group in the world,
because we've got the best songs and we haven't
even begun to show our potential yet.
Ian Brown 1990 •906

Anybody's first two albums
against my first two albums,
I'm there. I'm with The Beatles.

Noel Gallagher 1996. **No you're not** •907

I would hope we
mean more to people
than putting money
in a church basket
and saying ten Hail
Marys on a Sunday.
Has God played
Knebworth recently?

Noel Gallagher NME, 1997 •908

● *To the downright bonkers...*

I feel safe in white because, deep down inside, I'm an angel.

Puff Daddy •909

I don't exist. Tap my head and it
sounds like metal. I walk across
the sun and I don't cast a shadow.

Brett Anderson of Suede, 1994 •910

I don't go looking for weird shit, but it seems like it comes for me.

Gibby Haynes of Butthole Surfers •911

A lot of people think I'm clinically mad.

Morrissey 1986 •912

I'm naive in a Luke Skywalker way.
Not intuitive or smart enough to
be a Darth Vader. *Ryan Adams* of
Whiskeytown, 2001 •913

If I want a sound, I usually feel better if I've
chased it and killed it, skinned it and cooked it.
Tom Waits •914

It was only four tracks written on the machine,
but I was picking up twenty from the extra-terrestrial
squad. I am the dub shepherd. *Lee 'Scratch' Perry* •915

He was a freak and I was a freak,
so we decided to freak together.
Flea on Chili's bandmate Anthony Kiedis •916

I've got a very
irregular head.

Syd Barrett 1971 •917

Q: John, how would you describe yourself in one word?

Lennon: John. Another provocative answer during one of a number of
near-surreal interviews The Beatles give in San Francisco
during their 1964 tour of North America •918

260

I'm gonna give up playing piano.
I'm gonna become a rock and roll
suicide, take my nasty out and piddle
all over the front row, just to get rid
of my staid old image. *Elton John* 1974 •919

I wish people would turn off their computers,
go outside, talk to people, touch people,
lick people, enjoy each other's company
and smell each other on the rump. *Tre Cool* •920

We live on the 13th floor. Like most high-rise blocks
in America it doesn't have a thirteenth floor — 4,000
years of organised religion has tried to cover up the
fact that there are thirteen lunar months, and ladies
bleed thirteen times a year ... they want to take away
the number thirteen because they don't want nature
to impose itself. *Bjork* insists she's no fourteenth floor girl 2007 •921

The premise behind Oingo Boingo is to remain in a state of motion, bouncing — boinging along, if you will — and to try to present something that is fun and entertaining but also has a point of view. *Danny Elfman* **with his band's mission statement** •922

I'm just SO abstract. I'm so Jackson Pollock! Talking a load of old Pollocks. *Beth Orton* •923

Gwar was created by the master of creation, an ambiguous being named Larry, as the ultimate doomsday device. *Oderous Urungus* **delivers another mission statement** •924

I'm the artist formerly known as Beck. I have a genius wig. When I put that wig on, then the true genius emerges. I don't have enough hair to be a genius. I think you have to have hair going everywhere. *Beck* •925

We all had our childhoods, and we all know how important the balloon was. *Nena* **she of 99 of them, all red** •926

I love *ET* 'cos it reminds me of me. This person is like eight hundred years old and he's filling you with all kinds of wisdom. *Michael Jackson* •927

They're about to poke their genitals
into our cream cheese moon right
now. That's my eye; the moon is part
of me. Why don't they poke it in the
sun? They're not very daring.
Captain Beefheart's **take on the
moon landing in 1969** •928

I've seen fucking hundreds and
hundreds of spacecraft flying across
the sky over Salford. I mean hundreds
of them. There's obviously other planets
like this and other life. Anyone who
thinks there isn't is a dickhead.

The rational world of *Shaun Ryder* •929

When I'm no longer rapping, I want to open up
an ice cream parlour and call myself Scoop Dogg.
Snoop Dogg •930

I like to go to the graveyard, lay down
on somebody's grave, take a bottle out
there, dance around naked, y'know?

Tom Waits 1983 •931

There are only forty people in the world,
and five of them are hamburgers.

Captain Beefheart •932

I have a clairvoyant woman that I go
and see, and she told me that in my
last lifetime I was a Mohican Indian
and I had my brain removed.

Peter Gabriel 1974 •933

The stars are matter,
we're matter, but it
doesn't matter.

Captain Beefheart 1971 •934

I was outside the canopy of the earth, past the planets and into the stars, juiced up by some cosmic petrol-pump attendant. *Julian Cope* •935

Although I can see this world and a horrible situation, I also have a belief in other worlds. I'm just a believer of the fairies, I just feel the fairies in my stomach… I communicate with the fairies instinctively, I just hear things.

Tori Amos 1992 •936

They looked to me like they would be a great
rock band. I've only had to be right once.
Paul McGuinness **manager of U2** •937

We used to look at bands who could play better
and look better, and we used to say, 'They have
everything but it. We had nothing but it.' *Bono* •938

Rock 'n' roll is ridiculous. It's absurd. In the
past, U2 was trying to duck that. Now we're
wrapping our arms around it and giving it a
great big kiss. *Bono* •939

U2 is an original species... there are colours
and feelings and emotional terrain that we
occupy that is ours and ours alone. *Bono* •940

The rhythm section consists of
four people. The Edge is all four.
BB King **on working with U2** •941

What's special about U2 is the music, not the musician. I and the others are just ordinary people and our trade is to make music. Someone else's is to build houses or work in a factory or teach. We're just getting to grips with our trade as songwriters. *Bono* •942

We broke up the band after *War*. We literally broke up the band and formed another band with the same name and the same members. *Bono* •943

U2 are simple though, aren't they? I mean, I've said it before and I'll say it again, they're definitely simple. My window cleaner's got more to say than that cunt, let's face it. *Mark E. Smith* 1990 •944

When you're mega you can afford an independence that a lot of those so-called Indie bands can't. *Bono* •945

Being a rock star is like having a sex change. People stare at you, follow you down the street shouting comments, they hustle you and touch you up. I now know what it must feel like to be a woman. *Bono* 1992 •946

I never went to college, I've slept in some strange places, but the library wasn't one of them. I studied rock and roll and I grew up in Dublin in the 70s, music was an alarm bell for me, it woke me up to the world.

Bono on receiving an honorary doctorate from the University of Pennysylvania •947

My heroes are all alive. I never have worshipped at that altar of burnt-out youth.
Bono •948

When you sing, you make people vulnerable to change in their lives. You make yourself vulnerable to change in your life. But in the end, you've got to become the change you want to see in the world. *Bono* •949

In the Eighties we have to say that rock 'n' roll went to work for the corporation, and got up at six o'clock in the morning. *Bono* 1988 •950

It's not enough to rage against the lie… you've got to replace it with the truth.

Bono •951

I'm not in a position to be seen as a spokesman for a generation. I mean, how can you be a spokesman of a generation if you've nothing to say, other than 'Help!'
Bono attr •952

I do see myself as a modern prophet, it's true. Some people can't handle that.
Bono attr •953

268

Eight million people die every year for the price of going out with your friends to the movies and buying an ice cream. Literally for about $30 a head per year, you could save 8 million lives. Isn't that extraordinary? Preventable disease — not calamity, not famine, nothing like that. Preventable disease — just for the lack of medicines. That is cheap, that is a bargain.

Bono solves the world's problems •954

What a city, what a night, what a crowd, what a bomb, what a mistake, what a wanker you have for a President.

Bono acceptance speech at the MTV Europe Music Awards, referring to French nuclear testing in Pacific, 1996 •955

I actually didn't want him on the stage, 'cause his haircut at the time was so appalling.

Geldof on Bono at Live Aid •956

He's a poet. He's a philosopher. And last night, I think I saw him walking on water.

Mick Jagger on Bono, 1999 •957

Bono would love to be six foot tall and thin and good-looking. But he's not. He reminds me of a sodding mountain goat. *Ian McCulloch* •958

I don't understand what Bono… Is trying to tell us. Is it that the world is shit and false? Well I knew that already. Why is he always swaggering? Why that mock rock star arrogance? What's the concept? Why not just be a rock star and get on with it? *Paul Weller* in 1994. •959

After meeting Bono, it made me want to give up being in a rock and roll band.

Dave Grohl of Nirvana, 1992 •960

I am not frightened of dying, Anytime will do, I don't mind.

Quoted at the beginning of Great Gig In The Sky, from *Pink Floyd's* The Dark Side of the Moon, (1973) The voice is that of Gerry, the doorman at the Abbey Road Studios where Floyd were recording. •961

It's funny the way most people love
the dead. Once you are dead, you
are made for life. A prescient *Jimi Hendrix* •962

Now here is a young cat, extremely talented. For years, all the Negroes who'd
made it into the white market made it through servility, like Fats Domino,
a lovable, jolly fat image. Now here's this cat, you know — 'I am a super spade
man, I am like black and tough. And I will fuck you and rape you and do you in,
and I'm bad-assed and weird.' *Mike Bloomfield* **on Jimi Hendrix** •963

If I seem free,
it's because I'm
always running.

Jimi Hendrix •964

I'm the one that's got
to die when it's time
for me to die, so let
me live my life the
way I want to.
Jimi Hendrix •965

I don't think Jimi committed suicide in the
conventional way. He just decided to exit
when he wanted to. *Eric Burdon* **on Hendrix' suicide** •966

When they told me he was dead I felt fucking angry. I felt,
shit, he let me down. I felt betrayed even though it wasn't
a conscious decision for him to die. I felt like the loneliest
person on earth. *Eric Clapton* **on the death of Jimi Hendrix** •967

People, whether they know it or not, like
their blues singers miserable. They like
their blues singers to die afterwards.

Janis Joplin •968

Jim Morrison was possessed by a vision,
by a madness, by a rage to live, by an
all-consuming fire to make art. *Ray Manzarek* •969

I was and am a free spirit.
I wanted to gather information
and experience everything! To
get out and really live, not just
hang around the house and dream.

Marc Bolan •970

I'm very erratic but that's part of art and I consider myself
to be an artist, and I don't feel any compunction to be
professional if I don't feel like it, or play if I don't want to.
Marc Bolan 1974 •971

Don't worry, it's not loaded.

Last words of Chicago's *Terry Kath* before shooting himself in 1978 •972

We live in a country where John Lennon takes
six bullets to the chest and Yoko Ono is standing
next to him — no fucking bullet. Explain that to me.
Denis Leary **American comedian** •973

Rob: Liking both Marvin Gaye and Art Garfunkel is
like supporting both the Israelis and the Palestinians.
Laura: No, it's really not, Rob. You know why? Because
Marvin Gaye and Art Garfunkel make pop records.
Rob: Made. Made. Marvin Gaye is dead. His father shot him.
John Cusack **(Rob) and** *Iben Hjejle* **(Laura) in**
High Fidelity (2000) •974

I've only been in love with a beer bottle and a mirror.

Sid Vicious **Sounds, 1976** •975

Sid Vicious was just a mindless twerp.
I didn't find anything at all romantic
about him — or even interesting.
David Bowie **circa 1983** •976

274

Me live in the world but I'm not of the world.

Bob Marley •977

And it seems to me you lived your life
Like a candle in the wind.
Elton John Candle In The Wind
(with Bernie Taupin), (1973) from the album
Goodbye Yellow Brick Road. A song about
the fragile life of Marilyn Monroe •978

I was the first to know that Ian had died.
It was like a void, like someone had taken
a bridge out from under us. *Peter Hook* on the
death of Ian Curtis •979

You don't have cancer, it has you.

Ian Dury the week he died, April 2000 •980

The worst crime is faking it.
Kurt Cobain •981

If you die you're completely happy and
your soul somewhere lives on. I'm not
afraid of dying. Total peace after death,
becoming someone else is the best
hope I've got. *Kurt Cobain* •982

Thank you all from the pit of my burning, nauseous
stomach for your letters and concerns during the last
years. I'm too much of an erratic, moody person,
and I don't have the passion anymore.

from *Kurt Cobain's* suicide note, 1994 •983

Better to burn out
Than to fade away

Quoted on Kurt Cobain's suicide note; the line is
from *Neil Young* My My, Hey Hey (Out of the Blue),
from Rust Never Sleeps (1979). •984

I just wish Eddie Vedder would get on with it and kill himself.

Noel Gallagher of Oasis, 1996 •985

You're nobody til somebody kills you.
Notorious B.I.G. You're Nobody, (1997) **from the album**
Life After Death •986

It always happens, all the niggaz that change the world die, they don't get to die like regular people, they die violently.
Tupac Shakur •987

I believe that everything that you do bad comes back to you. So everything that I do that's bad, I'm going to suffer from it. But in my mind, I believe what I'm doing is right. So I feel like I'm going to heaven. *Tupac Shakur* •988

He was the perfect preservation against stuffiness and a lack of humanity.
David Johansen of the New York Dolls pays tribute to
Malcolm McLaren on his death in 2010 •989

We were supposed to be the alt-country Nirvana.
I guess I was supposed to hang myself with
a banjo string. *Ryan Adams* of Whiskeytown, 2000 •990

Poets usually have very
unhappy endings. Look
at Keats' life. Look at
Jim Morrison, if you want
to call him a poet. Look
at him. Although some
people say that he really
is in the Andes. *Bob Dylan* 1991 •991

Amy Winehouse, who was found dead on July 23rd aged twenty seven, ticked all the right boxes for a self-destructive wild child of pop, having bags of "attitude", a drink and drugs problem and a no-good man; yet underneath the ratty beehive hairdo, oversized plastic earrings, kohl-encrusted eyes and tattoo-covered arms, she was also an addictive and engaging performer with a natural contralto voice who sang with jazzy, passionate energy.

The Daily Telegraph obituary to the
late singer, 24th July, 2011. •992

Cocker, Jarvis •391, •493, •503, •687, •826; Cocteau Twins, The •881; *Cohen, Leonard* •721; *Cohn, Nik (rock writer)* •57, •73, •75, •80, •93, •100, •102, •226, •355; Coldplay •132; *Cole, Cheryl* •481, •482, •531; *Coleman, Ray (biographer)* •437; *Collier, Pat (of punk band* The Vibrators*)* •445; *Collins, Phil* •629, •633, •634; *Cooke, Sam* •60; *Cool, Tre (of* Green Day*)* •920; *Cooper, Alice* •180, •185; *Cope, Julian* •935; *Copeland, Stewart* •759; *Corgan, Billy* •39, •133, •201, •292, •904; *Costello, Elvis* •9, •119, •121, •165, •327, •465, •466, •472, •758; *Coward, Noel* •174; *Cowell, Simon* •652-655; *Coyne, Wayne (of* Flaming Lips*)* •774; *Crisp, Quentin* •593; *Crosby, David* •755; Culture Club •296, •452, •607; *Cuomo, Rivers (of* Weezer*)* •273; Cure, The •267; *Curtis, Ian* •517, •982; *D'Arby, Terence Trent* •320, •561, •900, •901; *Daltrey, Roger* •761; *Dammers, Jerry (of* The Specials*)* •98; *Dando, Evan* •293; *Davies, Ray* •70; *Deal, Kim (of* The Pixies*)* •533; *DeBurgh, Chris* •614; Deep Purple •202, •743; *Diddley, Bo* •48, •49; *Dido* •616; *Dion, Celine* •548, •631; Dire Straits •392; *Dirnt, Mike (of* Green Day*)* •275; *Doherty, Pete* •411, •412; *Domino, Fats* •963; *Donegan, Lonnie* •68; *Donnelly, Tanya (of* Belly*)* •41; Doors, The •333; *Dunckel, Jean-Benoit (of* Air*)* •448; Duran Duran •606; *Duritz, Adam (of* Counting Crows*)* •341, •762, •902; *Durst, Fred (of* Limp Bizkit*)* •206, •274; *Dury, Ian* •117, •824, •983; *Dylan, Bob* •88, •95, •97, •115, •147, •149, •329, •358,

•776-804, •1000; *Earle, Steve* •314, •818; East 17 •638; Echo & The Bunnymen •128; *Eddy, Duane* •115; *Edge, The* •84, •347, •812, •941; *Edwards, Rickey (of* Manic Street Preachers*)* •837; *Eitzel, Mark* •500; *Elfman, Danny* •922; *Elliott, Missy* •620; *Ellis-Bextor, Sophie* •645; *Elms, Robert (writer & DJ)* •592; *Emerson, Keith* •868, •869; Emerson, Lake & Palmer •867; *Eminem* •284-287, •349, •427; *Eno, Brian* •878; *Entwhistle, John* •176; *Epstein, Brian (*Beatles' *manager)* •134, •137-139; Erasure •664; *Etheridge, Melissa* •556; *Evans, Chris* •587; *Ezrin, Bob (producer)* •315; *Faithfull, Marianne* •222, •404, •514, •827; *Farrar, Jay (of* Son Volt*)* •742; *Farrell, Perry (of* Jane's Addiction*)* •419, •509; *Fat Boy Slim* •635; *Ferry, Bryan* •454, •876, •877; *Finn, Tim* •718; *Fitzgerald, Warren (of* The Vandals*)* •313; *Flea* •288, •430, •916; *Fogerty, John* •741; Frankie Goes To Hollywood •820; *Franklin, Aretha* •545; *Friend, Simon (of* The Levellers*)* •821; *Frischmann, Justine (of* Elastica*)* •202; *Froese, Edgar (of* Tangerine Dream*)* •898; *Frost, Jenny (of* Atomic Kitten*)* •665; *Fry, Martin (of* ABC*)* •609; *Furtado, Nelly* •773; *Gabriel, Peter* •702, •817, •933; *Gaga, Lady* •44, •656; *Gallagher, Liam* •130, •200, •371, •512; *Gallagher, Noel* •34, •123, •126, •127, •130, •271, •336, •352, •370, •644, •859, •907, •908, •992; *Garcia, Jerry* •40, •405, •864; *Garfunkel, Art* •976; *Gaye, Marvin* •886, •894, •976; *Gedge, Dave (of* The Wedding Present*)* •492, •763;